SAMS
Teach Yourself

MICROSOFT®
ACCESS 2000

Faithe Wempen

in 10 Minutes

SAMS

A Division of Macmillan Computer Publishing
201 West 103rd St., Indianapolis, Indiana, 46290 USA

SAMS TEACH YOURSELF MICROSOFT® ACCESS 2000 IN 10 MINUTES

Copyright © 1999 by Sams Publishing

International Standard Book Number:
0-672-31487-8

Library of Congress Catalog Card Number:
98-84937

Printed in the United States of America

First Printing: May 1999

01   00   4   3   2

TRADEMARKS

WARNING AND DISCLAIMER

EXECUTIVE EDITOR
Rosemarie Graham

ACQUISITIONS EDITOR
Neil Rowe

DEVELOPMENT EDITOR
Susan Shaw Dunn

MANAGING EDITOR
Jodi Jensen

SENIOR EDITOR
Susan Ross Moore

COPY EDITOR
Rhonda Tinch-Mize

INDEXER
Aamir Burki

PROOFREADERS
Eddie Lushbaugh
Maryann Steinhart

TECHNICAL EDITOR
Helen Feddema

TEAM COORDINATOR
Carol Ackerman

INTERIOR DESIGN
Gary Adair

COVER DESIGN
Aren Howell

LAYOUT TECHNICIANS
Brandon Allen
Stacey DeRome
Timothy Osborn
Amy Parker
Staci Somers

TABLE OF CONTENTS

INTRODUCTION   **1**

What Is Microsoft Access 2000? 1
What Is the *Sams Teach Yourself in 10 Minutes* Series? 2
Conventions Used in This Book 2

WHAT IS A DATABASE?   **4**

What Are Databases Good For? 4
How Access Stores Your Data 5
Reports 6
Queries 8
How the Parts Fit Together 8
Access Wizards Make Databases Easy 8

PLANNING YOUR DATABASE   **10**

Planning Is Important! 10
Determining the Tables You'll Need 11
What Forms Will You Use? 15
What Reports Will You Want to Produce? 16

STARTING AND EXITING ACCESS   **18**

Starting Access 18
Parts of the Screen 20
Exiting Access...21

USING THE HELP SYSTEM   **23**

Help: What's Available? 23
Asking Office Assistant 23
Using the Microsoft Access Help Window.................................28
Reading a Help Topic 31
Finding and Fixing Errors in the Program 32
Other Help Features 33

CREATING A NEW DATABASE   **34**

Choosing the Right Way to Create Your Database 34
Creating a Blank Database 35
Creating a Database with Database Wizard 37

SAVING, CLOSING, AND OPENING A DATABASE   41

Saving a Database 41
Closing a Database 42
Opening a Database 43
Changing the Drive or Folder..45
Finding a Database File 47

CREATING A TABLE WITH THE TABLE WIZARD   50

Why Create a Table?..50
Creating a Table Using the Table Wizard...51
Now What? 55

CREATING A TABLE WITHOUT A WIZARD   56

Why *Not* Use a Wizard? 56
Creating a Table in Table Design View 56
Understanding Data Types and Formats...59
Setting the Primary Key 61
Switching Between Design and Datasheet Views 62
Creating a Table by Entering Data 63

MODIFYING A TABLE   65

Editing Fields and Their Properties 65
Adding Fields 67
Deleting Fields 67
Hiding a Field..69
Deleting a Table 70

CREATING RELATIONSHIPS BETWEEN TABLES   71

Why Create Relationships?...71
Creating a Relationship Between Tables 72
What is Referential Integrity?...75
Editing a Relationship..76
Removing a Relationship 77
Now What? 77

ENTERING DATA INTO A TABLE   78

Entering a Record 78
Some Data-Entry Tricks 80
Moving Around in a Table 80

Printing a Table 81
Closing a Table 81

EDITING DATA IN A TABLE   83

Changing a Cell's Content 83
Selecting Records 85
Inserting New Records 86
Deleting Records..87
Moving and Copying Data 87

FORMATTING A TABLE   89

Why Format a Table? 89
Changing Column Width and Row Height........................89
Changing the Font..92

CREATING A SIMPLE FORM   94

Why Create Forms? 94
Creating a Form with AutoForm 95
Creating a Form with Form Wizard 96
Creating a Form from Scratch 98
Entering Data in a Form 102

MODIFYING A FORM   104

Cleaning Up Your Form: An Overview 104
Moving Controls..105
Moving Controls and Their Labels Independently..........106
Resizing Controls 107
Viewing Headers and Footers 108
Adding Labels..109
Formatting Controls 111
Changing Tab Order 113

CREATING SPECIAL DATA-ENTRY FIELDS ON A FORM 116

Why Use Special Data-Entry Controls?..........................116
What Kinds of Controls? 117
Creating a List Box or Combo Box 118
Creating an Option Group 120
Adding Command Buttons 123
Inserting ActiveX Controls 125

ADDING GRAPHICS TO FORMS   127

Why Add Graphics to Forms? 127
Importing Clip Art 127
Importing a Graphic 129
Resizing a Graphic 130
Creating a New Picture..131

SEARCHING FOR DATA   134

Using the Find Feature 134
Using the Replace Feature 137
Other Ways to Find Data 139

SORTING, INDEXING, AND FILTERING DATA   141

Finding and Organizing Your Data..141
Sorting Data 141
Filtering Data 143
Creating Indexes 146

CREATING A SIMPLE QUERY   148

What Can a Query Do?..148
Creating a Query Using the Simple Query Wizard 149
Printing Query Results 152
Other Query Wizards 153

DESIGNING YOUR OWN QUERY   155

Working with Query Design View 155
Adding Fields to a Query 157
Deleting a Field..158
Adding Criteria 159
Viewing Query Results 161

CUSTOMIZING A QUERY   162

Sorting a Field in a Query 162
Showing or Hiding a Field 163
Adding a Calculated Field 164

CREATING A SIMPLE REPORT   168

Why Create Reports? 168
Using AutoReport to Create a Report..168

Creating a Report with the Report Wizard 170
Viewing and Printing Reports in Print Preview 174

CUSTOMIZING A REPORT 175

Entering Report Design View 175
Working with Controls on Your Report 176

WORKING WITH RELATED TABLES 181

What Good Are Related Tables?...181
Viewing Related Data in Datasheet View...183
Creating Multitable Queries 183
Creating Multitable Forms 184
Creating Multitable Reports 187

CREATING A CHART 189

The Chart Advantage 189
Creating a Chart 189
Using Print Preview 194
Saving a Chart Report..194

USING ACCESS ON THE INTERNET 195

Some Internet Basics 195
Saving as a Web Page 196
Inserting Hyperlinks Into an Access Object 197
Creating Data Access Pages 201

SHARING YOUR DATABASE WITH OTHERS 204

Why Share Data? 204
Setting Up Exclusive Use 204
Assigning Passwords to Database Files 205
User-Level Security (Network Only) 206
Team Collaboration...207
Creating an .mde File 208
Encrypting a Database 210
Data Protection on Forms 211

IMPORTING AND EXPORTING DATA 213

Why Import and Export Data? 213
Importing Data from Other Programs 213
Exporting Data to Other Programs...219

BACKING UP YOUR DATA   221

Backing Up Your Database File 221
Repairing Damaged Database Files 222

INDEX   225

ABOUT THE AUTHOR

Faithe Wempen is the author of more than 30 computer books, including the best-selling *Microsoft Office 97 Professional 6-in-1*. She is the owner of Your Computer Friend, an Indianapolis-based computer training and troubleshooting business that specializes in helping beginning and intermediate-level users with their PCs.

DEDICATION

To Margaret.

ACKNOWLEDGMENTS

Most people don't know it, but a computer book is probably less than 50 percent the author's own handiwork. The rest of the credit belongs to the editors, formatters, layout technicians, managers, marketers, and salespeople who put the words and pictures into a good-looking package that people want to buy. Thanks to the top-notch editorial, production, marketing, and sales teams at Macmillan Publishing for another job well done.

TELL US WHAT YOU THINK!

As the reader of this book, *you* are our most important critic and commentator. We value your opinion and want to know what we're doing right, what we could do better, what areas you'd like to see us publish in, and any other words of wisdom you're willing to pass our way.

As an Associate Publisher for Sams Publishing, I welcome your comments. You can fax, email, or write me directly to let me know what you did or didn't like about this book—as well as what we can do to make our books stronger.

Please note that I cannot help you with technical problems related to the topic of this book, and that due to the high volume of mail I receive, I might not be able to reply to every message.

When you write, please be sure to include this book's title and author as well as your name and phone or fax number. I will carefully review your comments and share them with the author and editors who worked on the book.

Fax: 317-581-4770

Email: office_sams@mcp.com

Mail: Bradley L. Jones
                Associate Publisher
                Sams Publishing
                201 West 103rd Street
                Indianapolis, IN 46290 USA

INTRODUCTION

Congratulations on choosing Microsoft Access 2000! Access is one of the most powerful and flexible database management programs sold today. Whether you need a simple record of your home inventory or a complete business management system, Access can handle the job.

Although Access comes with many features to help beginners, it's still not a simple program. You probably won't be able to dive right in without instructions. But you certainly don't want to wade through a 500-page manual to find your way around!

- You want a clear-cut, plain-English introduction to Access.

- You need to create a professional-looking, usable database fast.

- You don't have time to study database theory.

- You need *Sams Teach Yourself Access 2000 in 10 Minutes*.

WHAT IS MICROSOFT ACCESS 2000?

Microsoft Access is a database management system, but I usually refer to it as a *database program* for short. This book covers Microsoft Access 2000, a version designed to work with Windows 95 or higher or Windows NT Workstation 3.51 or higher. It won't work on the 16-bit version of Windows (Windows 3.x).

Access enables you to collect, store, and arrange information as well as run reports that lead to conclusions. Here are just a few of the things you can do with Access:

- Type data directly into a database or import it from another program.

- Sort, index, and organize the way you want.

- Quickly create reports and mailing labels, using all or part of your data.

- Make customized data entry forms that simplify the way less experienced computer users enter new information in the database.

- Run queries that extract subsets of your data based on certain conditions.

 Installing Access   If you purchased Access as part of the Microsoft Office 2000 suite, you probably installed it when you installed the suite. If you haven't installed Microsoft Access, simply insert your installation CD into your PC and follow the onscreen prompts to do so.

WHAT IS THE *SAMS TEACH YOURSELF IN 10 MINUTES* SERIES?

The *Sams Teach Yourself in 10 Minutes* series is a new approach to learning computer programs. Rather than try to cover the entire program, these books teach you only about the features that beginners will most likely need.

No matter what your professional demands, *Sams Teach Yourself Access 2000 in 10 Minutes* will help you find and learn the main features of the program and become productive with it quickly. You can learn this wonderfully logical and powerful program in a fraction of the time you would normally spend learning a new program.

CONVENTIONS USED IN THIS BOOK

Each lesson in this book includes step-by-step instructions for performing a specific task. The following special boxes will help you along the way:

 Timesaver Tips   These offer shortcuts and hints for using the program most effectively.

Plain English   These identify new terms and definitions.

 Caution   These appear in places where new users often run into trouble.

Specific conventions in this book help you easily find your way around Microsoft Access:

- What you select or type appears in **bold, colored type**.

- Menu, Field, and Key names appear with the first letter capitalized.

LESSON 1
WHAT IS A DATABASE?

In this lesson, you will learn some basic database concepts and find out how Microsoft Access handles them.

WHAT ARE DATABASES GOOD FOR?

Strictly speaking, a *database* is any collection of information. Your local telephone book, for example, is a database, as is your Rolodex file and the card catalog at your local library. With a computerized database in Microsoft Access, you can store information, as with the three examples in this lesson, but you can also do much more. For instance, if you keep a list of all your business customers in an Access database, you can

- Print a list of all customers who haven't bought anything in the last 60 days, along with their phone numbers, so you can call each one.

- Sort the customers by ZIP code and print out mailing labels in that order. (Some bulk-mailing services require that you presort by ZIP code to get the cheaper mailing rate.)

- Create a simple onscreen order entry form that even your most technically unskilled employee can use successfully.

These examples only scratch the surface. With Access, you can manipulate your data in almost any way you can dream up.

HOW ACCESS STORES YOUR DATA

In Access, you first need to create a database file. That file holds everything you create for that database—not only all the data, but also the customized forms, reports, and indexes. If you have two or more businesses, you might want to create two or more separate databases, one for each business.

TABLES

The heart of each database is its tables. A table is a lot like a spreadsheet. Figure 1.1 shows a data table (or just *table* for short).

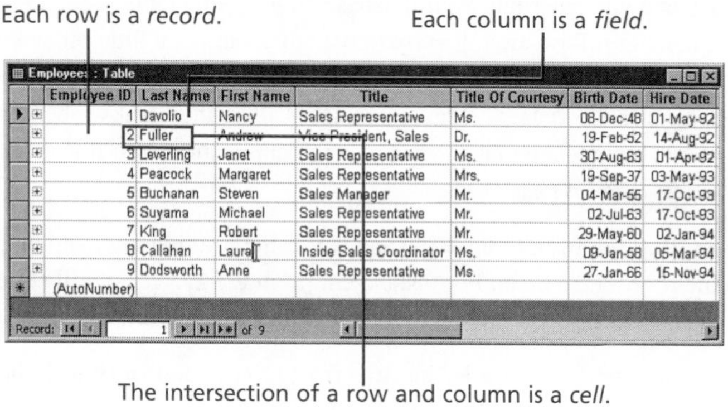

Each row is a *record.*   Each column is a *field.*

The intersection of a row and column is a *cell.*

FIGURE 1.1   A typical table in Access.

Access stores each database entry (for example, each employee or each inventory item) in its own row; this is a *record.* Each record is a collection of information about one thing—in this case, an employee. For example, all the information about Nancy Davolio, including Title, Birth Date, and Hire Date, forms a single record (refer to Figure 1.1).

Each type of detail is kept in its own column: a *field.* For example, Employee ID is one field, and Last Name is another. All the last names in the entire table are collectively known as the Last Name field.

At the intersection of a field and a row is the individual bit of data for that particular record; this area is a *cell*. For example, in the cell where the Birth Date column and the Nancy Davolio record intersect, you'll find 08-Dec-48, Nancy's birth date.

You'll learn how to create tables in Lessons 7 and 8. Each database file can have many tables. For instance, you might have a table that lists all your customers, and another table that lists information about the products you sell. A third table might keep track of your salespeople and their performance.

FORMS

All the data you enter into your database ends up in a table for storage. You can enter information directly into a table, but it's a little bit awkward to do so. Most people find it easier to create a special onscreen form in which to enter the data. A form resembles a fill-in-the-blanks sheet that you would complete by hand, such as a job application. You'll learn how to create a form in Lesson 15.

Access links the form to the table and stores the information that you put into the form in the table. For instance, in Figure 1.2, Access will store the employee data I'm entering on this form in the table shown in Figure 1.1.

The form shown in Figure 1.2 has two tabs; to view and work with the fields on the second page, simply click its tab.

 Multitable Forms   You can use a single form to enter data into several tables at once, as you'll learn in later lessons.

REPORTS

While forms are designed to be used onscreen, reports are designed to be printed. Reports are specially formatted collections of data, organized according to your specifications. For example, you might want to create a report of all your employees' sales performance (see Figure 1.3).

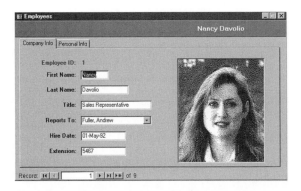

Figure 1.2   Forms make data entry more convenient.

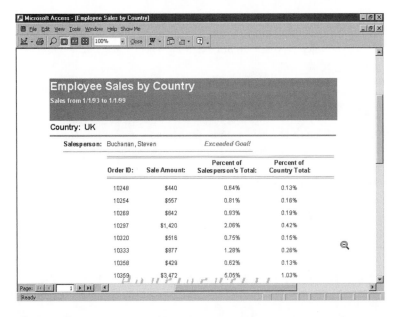

Figure 1.3   You can print this report and distribute it to your salespeople.

Print Preview   Although you create reports so that you can print them, you can also display them onscreen in Print Preview, as in Figure 1.3. You learn how to view and print reports in Lesson 24.

QUERIES

A *query* is a way of weeding out the information you don't want to see, so you can see the information you do need more clearly. You can think of it as a sieve you dump your data into; the data you don't want falls through the holes in the sieve, leaving only the data you're interested in.

Many people are afraid of queries because of the technical terms associated with them, such as *values, criteria,* and *masks.* But there's no need to be wary, as you learn in Lesson 21, where you create and use a simple query.

HOW THE PARTS FIT TOGETHER

Although you create tables, reports, forms, and queries in separate steps, they're all related. As mentioned earlier, tables are the central focus of all activities—all the other objects do something to or with the table data. Reports summarize and organize the table data; forms help you enter information into the table; queries help you find information you want to use in the table. In future lessons, you see how each part relates to the whole database.

ACCESS WIZARDS MAKE DATABASES EASY

Throughout this book, you will use Access's wizards. A *wizard* is a mini-program that "interviews" you, asking you questions about what you want to accomplish. It then takes your answers and creates the table, report, query, or whatever, according to your specifications. Figure 1.4 shows a sample wizard screen.

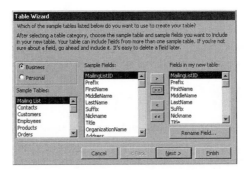

Figure 1.4   Wizards make it easy to create all kinds of database objects.

Each time you create a new object, such as a table or a form, you have the choice of creating it from scratch in Design view, or with a wizard to help you along. I recommend that all beginners use wizards as much as possible; I use them because they're so convenient. Leave the tough stuff, the Design view creations, to those with lots of leisure time.

In this lesson, you learned some basics about databases and Access. In Lesson 2, you will learn some strategies for planning your database. Don't skip Lesson 2! Ten minutes' worth of planning now can save you hours of backtracking later.

LESSON 2

PLANNING YOUR DATABASE

In this lesson, you will learn some principles of good database design to help you plan your course of action.

PLANNING IS IMPORTANT!

How many times have you dived enthusiastically into a new craft or skill without really knowing what you were doing? Your first attempt was probably pretty poor, whether the pursuit was pottery or computer programming. But as you worked, you probably made notes to yourself about what you'd do differently next time, and the next time you did better.

With something as important as a database, however, you can't afford to experiment through trial and error. In this lesson, I'll give you a crash course in the database planning principles that most people learn the hard way.

Before you create your database, you should ask the following questions:

- What data do I want to store, and what is the best way to organize it? This determines what tables you'll need.

- What data entry actions do I perform in the course of my business or hobby? This determines the forms you'll need.

- What information do I want to know about the status of the business or hobby? This answer tells you what reports and queries you'll want.

DETERMINING THE TABLES YOU'LL NEED

Technically, you need only one table, the minimum a database can function with. However, the biggest mistake most people make with Access is putting too much information in one table. Access is a relational database program; unlike simpler database programs, it's meant to handle many tables and create relationships among them. For example, in a database that keeps track of customer orders, you might have the following tables:

Customers	Customer Types
Orders	Shipping Methods
Payment Terms	Products
Salespeople	

 Plan Tables Now! You should plan your tables before you create your database because changing a table's structure after it's filled with data is difficult (but not impossible).

Another big mistake people make is trying to make each table look like a standalone report. For instance, they might repeat a customer's name and address in all eight tables because they want that information readily available when it's required. This is a waste! You can easily create a report or form that includes this information whenever you need it; it needs to appear in only one table.

NORMALIZING YOUR DATABASE

When a database suffers from poor table organization, experts say it's not *normalized*. Rules govern how a relational database should store its tables; these are the rules of data normalization.

> **Data Normalization**   Makes the tables as efficient and compact as possible to eliminate the possibility for confusion and error.

There are five normalization rules, but the last three are fairly complicated and used mostly by database professionals. In this lesson, I'll explain the first two normalization rules, which are all a beginner really needs to understand to avoid major mistakes.

> **Normalized Wizards**   Luckily, database professionals had a hand in creating Access's Database Wizard, so any tables you create with this feature (see Lesson 5) will be normalized.

1. AVOID REPEATED INFORMATION

Suppose that you want to keep contact information on your customers, along with a record of each transaction they make. If you kept it all in one table, you would have to repeat the customer's full name, address, and phone number each time you entered a new transaction. It would also be a nightmare if the customer's address changed; you would have to change the address in every transaction record for that customer.

Customer Name	Customer Address	Customer Phone	Order Date	Order Total
ABC Plumbing	201 W. 44th St.	(317) 555-2394	2/5/96	$155.90
ABC Plumbing	201 W. 44th St.	(317) 555-2394	5/14/96	$90.24
ABC Plumbing	201 W. 44th St.	(317) 555-2394	7/9/96	$224.50
Jack's Emporium	1155 Conner Ave.	(317) 555-4501	6/6/95	$1,592.99
Jack's Emporium	1155 Conner Ave.	(317) 555-4501	7/26/96	$990.41
Millie's Pizza	108 Ponting St.	(317) 554-2349	8/29/96	$39.95

A better way is to assign each customer an ID number. Include that ID number in a table that contains names and addresses; then use the same ID number as a link in a separate table that contains transactions.

Customers Table

Customer ID	Customer Name	Customer Address	Customer Phone
1	ABC Plumbing	201 W. 44th St.	(317) 555-2394
2	Jack's Emporium	1155 Conner Ave.	(317) 555-4501
3	Millie's Pizza	108 Ponting St.	(317)554-2349

Orders Table

Customer ID	Order Date	Order Total
1	2/5/96	$155.90
1	5/14/96	$90.24
1	7/9/96	$224.50
2	6/6/95	$1,592.99
2	7/26/96	$990.41
3	8/29/96	$39.95

2. AVOID REDUNDANT DATA

Suppose that you want to keep track of which employees have attended
certain training classes. There are may employees and lots of classes. One
way would be to keep it all in a single Personnel table, like this:

Employee Name	Employee Address	Employee Phone	Training Date	Class Taken	Credit Hours	Passed?
Phil Sharp	211 W. 16th St.	(317) 555-4321	5/5/96	Leadership Skills	3	Yes
Becky Rowan	40 Westfield Ct.	(317) 555-3905	5/5/96	Customer Service	2	Yes
Nick Gianti	559 Ponting St.	(317) 555-7683	6/15/96	Public Speaking	9	Yes
Martha Donato	720 E. Warren	(317) 555-2930	5/5/95	Public Speaking	9	No
Cynthia Hedges	108 Carroll St.	(317) 555-5990	6/15/96	Customer Service	2	Yes
Andrea Mayfair	3904 110th St.	(317) 554-0293	6/15/96	Leadership Skills	3	Yes

But what if an employee takes more than one class? You'd have to add a
duplicate line in the table to list it, and then you have the problem
described in the previous section—multiple records with virtually
identical field entries. What if the only employee who has taken a certain
class leaves the company? When you delete that employee's record, you
delete the information about the class's credit hours, too.

A better way would be to create separate tables for Employees, Classes,
and Training Done, like so:

Employee Table

Employee ID	Employee Name	Employee Address	Employee Phone
1	Phil Sharp	211 W. 16th St.	(317) 555-4321
2	Becky Rowan	40 Westfield Ct.	(317) 555-3905
3	Nick Gianti	559 Ponting St.	(317) 555-7683
4	Martha Donato	720 E. Warren	(317) 555-2930
5	Cynthia Hedges	108 Carroll St.	(317) 555-5990
6	Andrea Mayfair	3904 110th St.	(317) 555-0293

Class Table

Class ID	Class	Credits
C1	Leadership Skills	3
C2	Customer Service	2
C3	Public Speaking	9

Training Table

Employee ID	Date	Class	Passed?
1	5/5/96	C1	Yes
2	5/5/96	C2	Yes
3	6/16/96	C3	Yes
4	5/5/96	C3	No
5	6/15/96	C2	Yes
6	6/15/96	C1	Yes

SUMMARY: DESIGNING YOUR TABLES

Don't be overwhelmed by all this information about database
normalization. Good table organization boils down to a few simple
principles:

- Each table should have a theme—for instance, Employee
  Contact Information or Customer Transactions. Don't try to have
  more than one theme per table.

- If you see that you might end up repeating data in a table in the
  future, such as storing the customer's phone number in every
  purchase transaction, plan now to split the information that will
  be repeated into its own table.

- If you want to preserve a list of reference information (such as
  the names and credit hours for classes), put it in its own table.

- Wherever possible, use ID numbers, as they'll help you link tables later and avoid typing errors that come from entering long text strings (such as names) over and over.

- If you already have unique customer numbers or employee Social Security numbers, you can use them; otherwise, use an AutoNumber field to automatically generate a unique number for each record.

WHAT FORMS WILL YOU USE?

As explained in Lesson 1, forms are data-entry tools. You can arrange fields from several tables on a form and easily enter data into those fields on a single screen. For instance, a customer order form might include information from the Orders table and the Products table (see Figure 2.1).

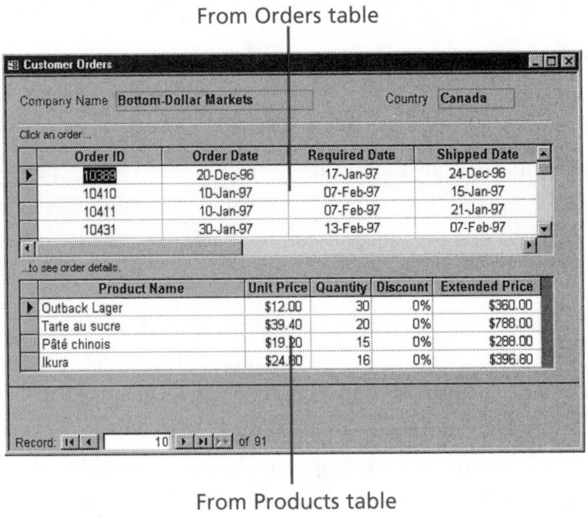

From Orders table

From Products table

FIGURE 2.1 A form can be the link between several tables.

When thinking about what forms you'll need, the question is really about what actions you will perform. The following list describes some actions that might require a form:

- Hiring employees (and entering their information in the database)

- Selling goods or services

- Making purchases

- Collecting the names and contact information for volunteers

- Keeping track of inventory

 I Can't Predict What Forms I'll Need!   Although it's important to have effective forms, you can make changes to forms at any time fairly easily (unlike tables), so you don't have to know exactly what forms you want before you start. You learn to create forms in Lesson 15.

WHAT REPORTS WILL YOU WANT TO PRODUCE?

A report satisfies your need for information about your data. It's usually printed (unlike tables and forms, which are usually used onscreen). For instance, you might want a report of all people who haven't paid their membership dues, or all accounts with a balance owed of more than $1,000. (You can find this information with a query, too, as you learn in Lesson 21.)

A report is usually for the benefit of other people who aren't sitting with you at your computer. For instance, you might print a report to hand out to your board of directors to encourage them to keep you on as CEO. A report can pull data from many tables at once, perform calculations on the data (such as summing or averaging), and present you with neatly formatted results. Here are some things you can do with reports:

- Print a list of all your personal possessions with a replacement value over $50, for insurance purposes

- Show a listing of all club members who haven't paid their dues

- Calculate and show the current depreciated value of all capital equipment

- List the commissions paid to each of your top 50 salespeople in the last quarter, compared with the company-wide average

You can create new reports at any time; you don't have to plan them before you create your database. However, if you know you will want a certain report, you might design your tables in the format that will be most effective for that report's use.

In this lesson, you planned your database tables, forms, and reports. In the next lesson, you will learn how to start and exit Access.

LESSON 3

STARTING AND EXITING ACCESS

In this lesson, you will learn how to start and exit Microsoft Access.

STARTING ACCESS

You can start Access in several ways, depending on how you've installed it. One way is to use the Start menu button. Follow these steps:

1. Click the **Start** button. A menu appears.

2. Highlight or point to **Programs**. A list of your program groups appears, with a list of separate Microsoft applications under the groups.

3. Click **Microsoft Access** in the list of applications. Access starts.

 Moving Programs Around on the Start Menu   If you would prefer to have Access in a different program group, open the Start menu and drag the Access item to another location of your choice.

OTHER WAYS TO START ACCESS

Some other ways to start Access require more knowledge of Windows and Microsoft Office. If you're confused by them, stick with the primary method explained in the preceding section.

- You can create a shortcut icon for Access to sit on your desktop; you can then start Access by double-clicking the icon. To create the shortcut icon, drag the Access item from the Start menu to the desktop.

- When you're browsing files in Windows Explorer, you can double-click any Access data file to start Access and open that data file. Access data files have an .mdb extension and a little icon next to them that resembles the icon next to Microsoft Access on the Programs menu.

- If you can't find Access, you can search for it. Click the **Start** button and select **Find**, select **Files or Folders**, and then type **msaccess.exe** in the **Named** text box. Open the **Look In** list and select **My Computer**. Then click **Find Now**. When the file appears on the list at the bottom of the Find window, double-click it to start Access, or right-click and drag it to the desktop to create an Access shortcut.

When you start Access, the first thing you'll see is a dialog box prompting you to create a new database or open an existing one (see Figure 3.1). For now, click **Cancel**. (We won't be working with any particular database in this lesson.)

FIGURE **3.1**   This Microsoft Access dialog box appears each time you start Access.

PARTS OF THE SCREEN

Access is much like any other Windows program: It contains menus, toolbars, a status bar, and so on. Figure 3.2 points out these landmarks. Notice that in Figure 3.2, many of the toolbar buttons are grayed out (which means you can't use them right now). There's also nothing in the work area, because no database file is open. The Access screen will become a much busier place in later lessons when you begin working with a database; the buttons will become available, and your database will appear in the work area.

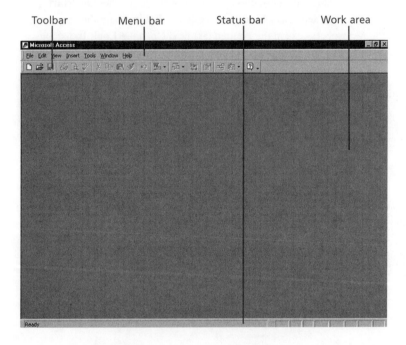

FIGURE 3.2   Access has the same interface landmarks as any Windows program.

UNDERSTANDING ACCESS TOOLBARS

If you've used Windows programs before, you're probably familiar with *toolbars*—rows of buttons that represent common commands you can issue. Toolbar buttons are often shortcuts for menu commands.

The Access toolbar changes depending on which type of database object you're working with at the time (table, form, and so on), and what you're doing to it. More toolbars sometimes appear when you're doing special activities, such as drawing. To find out what a toolbar button does, put your mouse pointer over it; its name appears next to the pointer (see Figure 3.3). This feature is a *ToolTip* (or a *ScreenTip*); you can use ToolTips even when a button is unavailable (grayed out).

Button name   Close button

Figure 3.3   To find out what a toolbar button does, point at it.

 Customizing Toolbars   You can choose which toolbars you view at any time, and even add and remove buttons from a toolbar. If you right-click any toolbar, a shortcut menu appears. You can select a toolbar for viewing from that list, or click Customize to open a dialog box where you can customize any toolbar.

EXITING ACCESS

When you finish working with Access, you should exit it to free up your computer's memory for other tasks. You can exit Access in several ways:

- Press **Alt+F4**.

- Select **File, Exit**.

- Click the Access window's Close (×) button (refer to Figure 3.3).

Alt+F4? File, Exit?   In this book, I use a kind of shorthand to tell you what keys to press and which menu commands to select. When you see press Alt+F4, it means hold down the Alt key on the keyboard while you press the F4 key. When you see select File, Exit, it means click the word File on the menu bar, and then click the Exit command on the menu that appears.

In this lesson, you learned how to start and exit Access, and about the main parts of the screen, including the toolbar buttons. In the next lesson, you will learn how to use Access's Help system.

Lesson 4

Using the Help System

In this lesson, you learn about the various types of help available to you in Access.

Help: What's Available?

Because every person is different, Access offers many ways to get help with the program. You can

- Ask the Office Assistant for help.

- Get help on a particular element you see onscreen with the What's This? tool.

- Choose what you're interested in learning about from a series of help topics.

- If you're connected to the Internet, access Microsoft's On the Web feature to view Web pages containing help information.

Asking Office Assistant

You've probably already met the Office Assistant—it's Clippit, the paperclip that pops up to give you advice. Don't let its whimsical appearance fool you, though; behind the Office Assistant is a very powerful Help system.

DISPLAYING OR HIDING THE OFFICE ASSISTANT

By default, the Office Assistant is turned on and sits on top of whatever you're working on. You can turn it off by right-clicking it and choosing **Hide** (see Figure 4.1). If the Office Assistant is ever in your way but you don't want to hide it, drag it with your mouse to a different spot onscreen.

Office Assistant

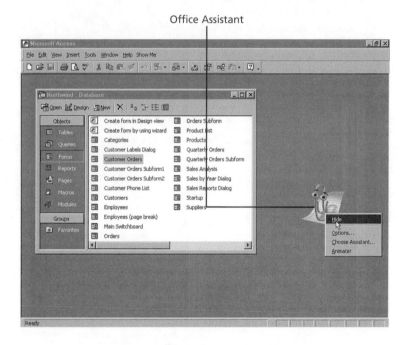

FIGURE 4.1   The Office Assistant sits on top of the Access window.

 To redisplay the Office Assistant, choose **Help, Show the Office Assistant** or click the Microsoft Access Help button on the toolbar.

 More Assistants Available   Notice on the shortcut menu in Figure 4.1 that you can select Choose Assistant to choose a different character (if you don't like talking office supplies, for instance).

The Kinds of Help Office Assistant Provides

When you click the Office Assistant, a bubble appears next to (or above) its box asking you what kind of help you want (see Figure 4.2). You can do any of the following:

- Type a question in the text box provided to tell the Office Assistant what kind of help you need, and then click **Search**. (More on this shortly.)

- Click the **Options** button to customize the way the Office Assistant works. (I'll explain more about this later in this lesson.)

- Click away from the bubble to close the bubble (but leave the Office Assistant onscreen).

FIGURE 4.2   Office Assistant at your service, asking what you need help with.

If you close the help bubble, you can reopen it at any time by clicking the **Help** button on the Standard toolbar; by pressing **F1**; by selecting **Help**, **Microsoft Access Help**; or by clicking the Office Assistant.

> **Extra Tips Along the Way**   Sometimes you'll see a light bulb over the Office Assistant's head. This means that the Office Assistant has a suggestion for you regarding the task that you're now performing. To get the suggestion, just click the light bulb.

ASKING THE OFFICE ASSISTANT A QUESTION

If you need help on a particular topic, simply type a question into the text box shown in Figure 4.2. Follow these steps:

1. If the Office Assistant's help bubble doesn't appear, click the Office Assistant or press **F1**.

2. Type a question into the text box. For instance, you might type **How do I print a table?** to get help printing your data.

3. Press **Enter** or click the **Search** button. The Office Assistant provides some topics that might match what you're looking for. For instance, Figure 4.3 shows the Office Assistant's answer to the question "How do I print a table?"

FIGURE **4.3**   The Office Assistant asks you to narrow exactly what you are trying to accomplish, so it can provide the best help possible.

4. Click the option that best describes what you're trying to do. For instance, I'm going to choose **Print the datasheet of a table, query, or form** from Figure 4.3. A Help window appears with instructions for the specified task.

   If none of the options describe what you want, click the **See more** arrow to view more options, or type a different question in the text box.

5. If another list of topics appears, click a link to further narrow the help you want.

6. Read the instructions that appear. Then close the Microsoft Access Help window (× button) or click the Office Assistant again and search for something else.

For more information about working with the Microsoft Access Help window, see "Using the Microsoft Access Help Window" later in this lesson.

Turning Off the Office Assistant Feature

By default, whenever you access the Help system in Access, you do so using the Office Assistant. Some people, however, just can't stand dealing with a cartoon character, or are more advanced users who want more power and flexibility in using the Help system. If that's you, you can turn the Office Assistant off altogether:

1. Right-click the Office Assistant and choose **Options.**

2. In the Office Assistant dialog box that appears, deselect the **Use the Office Assistant** check box.

3. Click **OK.**

When you turn off the Office Assistant, all the normal ways of activating the assistant (**F1**, the **Help, Microsoft Access Help** command, and so on) activate the Microsoft Access Help window instead.

USING THE MICROSOFT ACCESS HELP WINDOW

As soon as the Microsoft Access Help window is open (from one of the Office Assistant's searches), you can browse the Help system on your own. If you have used an earlier version of a Microsoft Office product, you might be familiar with the Contents, Index, and Find mechanisms that used to be the hallmark of a Microsoft product's Help system. These are still available in Office 2000 programs such as Access, but in a slightly different form.

If you're using an Office Assistant, the only way to get into the main Help system is by asking a question, as you learned to do earlier in this lesson. If you turn off the Office Assistant, however, as explained in the preceding section, choosing **Help, Microsoft Access Help** accesses the Help system directly.

If you're using the Help system from an Office Assistant query, click the **Show** button (the leftmost button) in the Help window's toolbar to expand the Help controls you'll need in the following sections. This button becomes the Hide button when the help controls are shown, so I refer to it as the Show/Hide button in upcoming sections.

CONTENTS

The **Contents** page of the Help system is a series of folders you can open, similar to the folder pane of Windows Explorer. Each folder has one or more Help topics in it. Figure 4.4 shows this page.

To select a Help topic from the Contents screen, follow these steps:

1. If you don't see the tabbed sections shown in Figure 4.4, click the **Show** button on the Help window's toolbar.

2. Click the **Contents** tab.

3. Find the folder that describes, in broad terms, what you're looking for help with.

4. Double-click the folder, or click its plus sign. A list of Help articles appears below the folder (see Figure 4.4).

5. Click a Help article to display it in the right pane.

6. After reading that article, display and read another or close the Help system by clicking its Close (×) button.

Show/Hide button   The help articles appear here to be read.

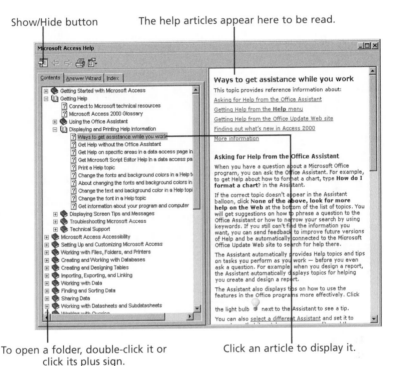

To open a folder, double-click it or   Click an article to display it.
click its plus sign.

FIGURE 4.4   The Help Contents window is a group of folders that contain Help information.

INDEX

The Index is an alphabetical listing of every Help topic available. It's similar to an index in a book. To use the Index, follow these steps:

1. If you don't see the tabbed pages in the Help window, click the **Show** button on the Help window's toolbar.

2. Click the **Index** tab.

3. Type the first few letters of the topic you want to find. The index list jumps quickly to that spot.

4. Click the **Search** button or press **Enter**. A list of topics (articles) appears that include the chosen keyword (see Figure 4.5).

Type a word here.   The list jumps to match (as closely as   Topics found
                      possible) what you typed.   appear here.

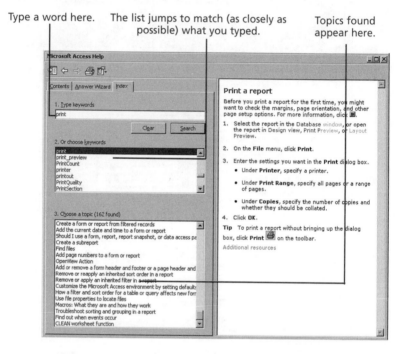

FIGURE 4.5   Browse through topics alphabetically with the Index.

5. Click a topic to display it.

6. After reading an article, display and read another or close the Help system by clicking its Close (×) button.

ANSWER WIZARD

The Answer Wizard is comparable to the Office Assistant, except without the cartoon character. You can ask it a question in ordinary language, just as you can the Office Assistant.

To use the Answer Wizard, follow these steps:

1. If you don't see the tabbed sections in the Help window, click the **Show** button on the Help window's toolbar.

2. Click the **Answer Wizard** tab.

3. Type your question in the **What would you like to do?** box, and click **Search**, or press Enter.

4. Browse through the topics that appear in the bottom box, and click the one that matches the help you need (see Figure 4.6).

5. After reading the article, display and read another or close the Help system by clicking its Close (×) button.

READING A HELP TOPIC

No matter which avenue you choose for finding a help topic (the Office Assistant, Contents, Index, or Answer Wizard), you eventually end up at an article you can read, similar to the one in the right-hand pane of Figure 4.6. From here, you can read the information onscreen or do any of the following:

- Click a blue word to see a definition of it.

- Click a >> button or an underlined word to jump to another Help screen.

- Print a hard copy of the information by clicking the **Print** button on the Help window's toolbar.

- Copy the text to the Clipboard (for pasting into a program such as Microsoft Word or Windows Notepad) by highlighting the text to copy and pressing **Ctrl+C**.

- Return to the previous Help topic you viewed by clicking the **Back** button. (If you haven't looked at other Help topics this session, the Back button isn't available.)

- Close the Help window by clicking its Close (×) button.

Type your question.   Print button   Options button

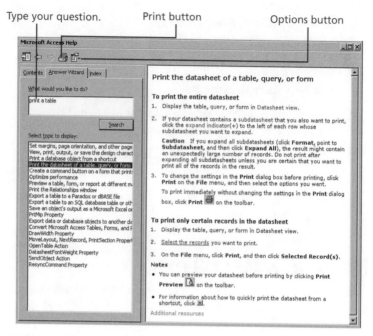

Figure 4.6 Use the Answer Wizard to locate all the Help topics that deal with a certain subject.

FINDING AND FIXING ERRORS IN THE PROGRAM

A new feature in Office 2000 is Detect and Repair. It can identify problems with your copy of Access, such as a damaged program file or corrupted driver, and repair the problem by using your original Office 2000 or Access 2000 disk. This repair process can take a long time (30 minutes or more), so don't perform it unless you suspect problems.

If Access starts behaving strangely, the best thing to do is close Access and restart Windows. If you are still having trouble, follow these steps:

1. Choose **Help, Detect and Repair**.

2. An explanation box appears. Click **Start**.

3. Wait for the utility to compare all your Access files to the original ones on the CD, to check for errors. Be patient; this takes a long time.

4. When you see a message that says you must restart the system for the changes to take effect, click **Yes**.

OTHER HELP FEATURES

Let's finish up this lesson by looking at a few of the Help features that you might not use as frequently but still can be very useful.

GETTING HELP WITH SCREEN ELEMENTS

If you wonder what a particular button or tool onscreen is used for, wonder no more. Just follow these steps:

1. Select **Help, What's This?** or press **Shift+F1**. The mouse pointer changes to a question mark pointer.

2. Click the screen element for which you want help. A box appears explaining the element.

GETTING MORE HELP ON THE WEB

Whenever you use the Office Assistant, one choice on the second "page" of search results (which you display by clicking **See more**) is **None of the above, look for more help on the Web.** If you choose that, and you have an Internet connection, Internet Explorer opens and jumps to the Microsoft Web site, where you can look up more information.

You can also go to the Microsoft Web site without having a particular question in mind by selecting **Help,** Microsoft on the Web.

In this lesson, you learned about the many ways that Access offers help. In the next lesson, you will learn about the different views Access offers for working with your database.

LESSON 5

CREATING A NEW DATABASE

In this lesson, you will learn how to create a blank database. You also will learn how to create a database with pre-made tables, reports, and forms with the database wizard.

CHOOSING THE RIGHT WAY TO CREATE YOUR DATABASE

Before you create your database, you have an important decision to make: should you create a blank database from scratch, and then manually create all the tables, reports, and forms you'll need, or should you use a database wizard, which does all that for you?

 Database Wizard Access comes with several database wizards. These are mini-programs that interview you about your needs and then create a database structure that matches them. (You will enter the actual data yourself.)

The answer depends on how well the available wizards match your needs. If a database wizard is close to what you want, it's quickest to use it to create your database, and then modify it as needed. (Of course, you won't know what wizards are available until you open the list of them, as you'll see later in this lesson.) If you're in a hurry, using a wizard can save you lots of time.

On the other hand, if you want a special-purpose database that isn't similar to any of the wizards, or if you're creating the database primarily as a training exercise for yourself, you should create the blank database.

CREATING A BLANK DATABASE

Creating a blank database is very simple because you're just creating an outer shell at this point, without any tables, forms, and whatnot. If you just started Access and the Microsoft Access dialog box is still displayed (see Figure 5.1), follow these steps:

1. Click **Blank Access database.**

2. Click **OK.** The File New Database dialog box opens.

3. Type a name for the new file in the **File Name** text box, and then click **Create.** Access creates the new database.

FIGURE **5.1**   When you first start Access, you can start a new database quickly from the Microsoft Access dialog box.

After you close the initial dialog, you can't get it back until you exit and restart Access. But you don't need it to start a new database; at any time you can follow these steps:

1. Select **File, New,** or click the **New** button on the toolbar. The New dialog box appears (see Figure 5.2).

2. Make sure the **General** tab is on top by clicking it. Double-click the **Database** icon. The File New Database dialog box appears.

3. Type a name for your new database (preferably something descriptive) in the **File name** text box. For example, I typed

Kennel Records. Then click **Create**. Access creates the new database by default in the My Documents folder.

Figure 5.2   The New dialog box's different tabs give you options to create different kinds of databases.

Your database is completely blank at this point, and you see the database's window, open to the Tables section (see Figure 5.3).

Figure 5.3   A new database window.

Each item listed in the Objects section of Figure 5.3 represents a different kind of object you can create in a database. Later, you learn how to create tables (Lessons 7 and 8), forms (Lesson 14), queries (Lesson 20), and reports (Lesson 23).

Object Shortcuts   The object shortcuts (such as Create table in Design view) aren't necessary—you can create a new database object by simply clicking the **New** toolbar button. If you tire of these shortcuts and want to conserve list space for your own database objects, you can turn them off by choosing **Options** from the **Tools** menu, and deselecting the **New object shortcuts** option.

CREATING A DATABASE WITH DATABASE WIZARD

A database wizard can create almost all the tables, forms, and reports you will ever need, automatically. The trick is choosing the right wizard to suit your purpose. Follow these steps:

1. If you just started Access and the Microsoft Access dialog box is still onscreen, click **Access database wizards, pages, and projects**, and then click **OK**. Or, if you've already closed the dialog box, select **File, New**. Either way, the New dialog box appears.

2. If it's not already on top, click the **Databases** tab to display the list of wizards.

3. Click one of the database wizards (the icons with the magic wands across them). For this example, I'll choose **Contact Management**.

4. When you've selected the wizard you want, click **OK**. The File New Database dialog box appears.

5. Type a name for the database, and then click **Create** to continue. The wizard starts, and some information appears explaining what the wizard does.

6. Click **Next** to continue. A list of the tables to be created appears (see Figure 5.4). The tables appear on the left, and the selected table's fields are on the right.

Fields in the selected table.
Optional fields (in italic).

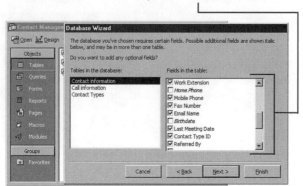

FIGURE **5.4**   This wizard creates these tables and fields automatically for you.

7. Click a table and examine its list of fields. Optional fields are in italics. To include an optional field, click it to place a check mark next to it. Click **Next** to continue.

I Don't Want These Tables and Fields!   Sorry, that's the price you pay for going with a prefabricated wizard. You can't deselect any fields except the optional (italicized) ones. But you can delete the tables and fields you don't want later. See Lesson 9 to learn how to delete individual fields or an entire table. If the tables and fields appear totally inappropriate, perhaps you're using the wrong wizard for your needs; click **Cancel** and try another.

8. The wizard asks you what kind of screen display style you want. Click a display style in the list and examine the preview of the style that appears. After you decide on a style, click it, and then click **Next**.

9. The wizard asks you for a style for printed reports. Click a report style and examine the preview of it. When you decide on a style, click it, and then click **Next**.

Report Background The colored backgrounds used for some report styles look nice onscreen, but they don't print well on a black-and-white printer. Stick to plain backgrounds for the best report printouts.

10. The wizard asks what title you want for the database. This title appears on reports and can be different from the file name. Enter a title (see Figure 5.5).

Click here to   See your picture choices
include a picture.   by clicking this button.

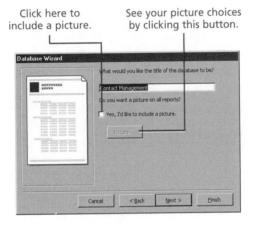

FIGURE 5.5   Enter a title for the database, and optionally, choose a graphic to use for a logo.

11. (Optional) To include a picture on your forms and reports (for example, your company's logo), click the **Yes, I'd like to include a picture** check box. Then click the **Picture** button, choose a picture file (change the drive or folder if needed), and click **OK** to return to the wizard.

12. Click **Next** to continue. Then, at the Finish screen, click **Finish** to open the new database. The wizard goes to work creating your database. (It might take several minutes.)

When the database is finished, the Main Switchboard window appears (see Figure 5.6). The Switchboard opens automatically whenever you open the database.

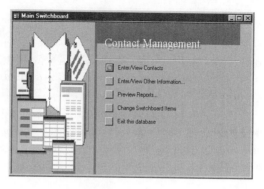

FIGURE 5.6   The Switchboard window is an extra bonus provided by the database wizards.

All the databases created by a database wizard include the Main Switchboard, which is nothing more than a fancy form with some programming built in. It lets you perform common tasks with the database by clicking a button. We won't be working with the Main Switchboard, so just click the Main Switchboard window's Close (×) button to get rid of it.

 I Hate That Switchboard!   To prevent the Switchboard from opening when you open the database, choose **Tools, Startup.** Open the **Display Form** drop-down list, and select **[None]. Click OK.**

After you close the Switchboard window, you see the database window. If it's minimized, double-click its title bar (bottom left corner of the screen) to reopen it. Click the **Tables** object type, and you see that several tables have been created for you. Click the other object types to see the other objects created as well.

Although you might have all the tables, reports, and forms you need, you might still want to go through the lessons in this book in chronological order, to learn about creating and modifying these objects. If you're in a hurry to enter data, though, skip to Lesson 11, where you'll learn how to enter data in a table, or the end of Lesson 14, where you'll learn about data entry on a form.

In this lesson, you learned to create a database from scratch and use a database wizard. In the next lesson, you will learn how to save, close, and open a database.

LESSON 6

SAVING, CLOSING, AND OPENING A DATABASE

In this lesson, you will learn how to save your database, close it, and reopen it. You also will learn how to find a misplaced database file.

SAVING A DATABASE

You need to save your work so that you don't lose anything you've typed after you turn off the computer or close Access.

When you created the database, you saved it in Lesson 5 by naming it. When you enter each record, Access automatically saves your work. (You learn how to enter records in Lesson 11.) You don't need to save your work until you're ready to close your database.

When you change the structure of a table, form, or other object, Access won't let you close that object or close the database without confirming whether you want to save your changes. You'll see a dialog box like the one in Figure 6.1; just click **Yes** to save your changes. (If you have the Office Assistant enabled, the same question appears in a thought bubble over its head instead of in a dialog box.)

FIGURE 6.1 When you change an object's structure, Access asks whether it should save your changes.

Notice that the Save and Save As commands on the File menu aren't even available most of the time; they're grayed out. When you have a particular object highlighted in the database window, such as a table, the Save As and Export commands are available. You can use the Save As command to save your table in a different format (such as saving a table as a report). The Export command lets you save an object in an external file format that another program (such as Excel) can read.

Using Tables in Other Programs   Another way to copy a table to another application or another database is with the Copy and Paste commands. Highlight the table in the Database window and select **Edit, Copy.** Then open a different database or application and select **Edit, Paste.** A dialog box opens, which might give you the options of pasting the table structure only or the structure plus its data. You can also choose to append the data to existing tables, if the fields match up.

CLOSING A DATABASE

When you finish working with a database, close it. When you finish using Access, just exit the program (see Lesson 3), and the database closes along with the program. If you want to close the database and then open another, however, do any of the following (see Figure 6.2):

- Double-click the Control-menu icon (in the top-left corner) for the database.

- Click the database window's Close (✕) button (the top right corner).

- Select **File, Close.**

- Press **Ctrl+F4.**

- Press **Ctrl+W** (if the database window is the active window).

- Click the database window's **Open** button to close the current database and open a new one.

Select Close
from the File
menu.

Click here.

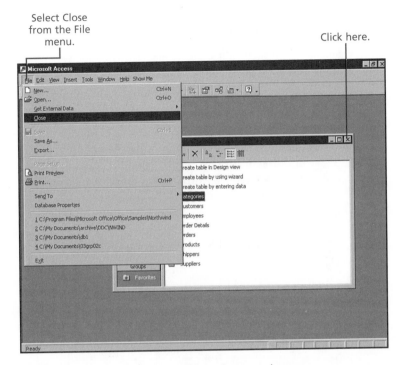

FIGURE 6.2 You can close a database in several ways.

 Can I Have More Than One Database Open? Sure, you can. In fact, you might want several open, so you can transfer data between them. However, if your computer is short on memory (less than 16MB), you'll find that Access runs faster when you close all files that you're not using.

OPENING A DATABASE

When you start Access the next time you want to use your database, you won't create a new one from scratch, of course, as you did in Lesson 5. You'll open your existing one.

The easiest way to open a database you've recently used is to select it from the File menu. Follow these steps:

1. Open the **File** menu. You'll see up to nine databases you've recently used listed at the bottom of the menu.

2. Click the database you want to open.

Want to see more files?   To increase the number of files displayed in this list, select a number up to 9 in the **Recently Used Files** drop-down list on the **General** tab of the Options dialog box (**Tools, Options**).

If the database you want to open isn't listed, you need to use the following procedure instead:

1. Select **File, Open,** or click the toolbar's **Open** button. The Open dialog box appears (see Figure 6.3).

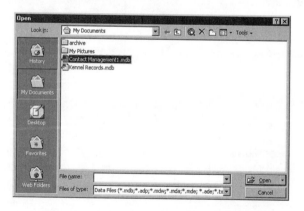

FIGURE 6.3   Open a different database file with this dialog box.

2. If the file isn't in the currently displayed folder, change drives and folders. Refer to the next section, "Changing the Drive or Folder."

3. Double-click the file to open it.

New Feature In Access 2000, the **Open** button in the Open dialog box has a drop-down list. From it, you can choose (in addition to the standard Open choice) Read-Only, **Open Exclusive**, or **Open Exclusive Read Only. Open Read-Only** prevents changes from being saved to the database, **Open Exclusive** prevents another user from working on the database while you have it open, and **Open Exclusive Read Only** does both. Any of these selections helps prevent inadvertent changes to a valuable database.

CHANGING THE DRIVE OR FOLDER

The dialog boxes for opening (and saving) files in Office 2000 programs are different from the ones in Windows 95/98 in general. The Open and Save As dialog boxes take a bit of getting used to.

To change to a different drive, you must open the **Look In** or **Save In** drop-down list. (The name changes depending on whether you're saving or opening a file.) Figure 6.4 shows this drop-down list in the Open dialog box. From it, choose the drive that contains the file you want to open.

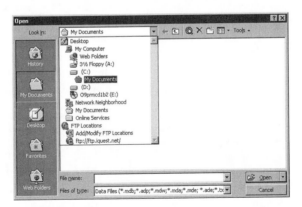

FIGURE 6.4   Use this drop-down list to choose a different drive.

Next, you must select the folder where you want to save the file (or open it from). When you select the drive, a list of the folders on that drive appears. Double-click the folder you want to select.

Table 6.1 explains the buttons and other controls you see in the Save As and Open dialog boxes.

TABLE 6.1   BUTTONS FOR CHANGING DRIVES AND FOLDERS IN WINDOWS 95 DIALOG BOXES

CONTROL	PURPOSE
	Moves back to the previous folder you looked at, if there is one. Otherwise, this button is unavailable.
	Moves to the folder "above" the one shown in the Save In box (that is, the folder in which the current database resides).
	Opens Internet Explorer, so you can search the Web for a file (seldom used).
	Deletes the selected file.
	Creates a new folder.
	Opens a list of viewing options for the file list (List, Details, Properties, and Preview), plus an Arrange Icons submenu where you can arrange icons by Name, Type, Size, or Date.
Tools	Opens a menu of commands you can issue for the selected file (Find, Delete, Rename, and others).

In addition to the buttons across the top of the Save As and Open dialog boxes, there are also shortcut icons along the left side. These point to folders that some people use to store files or shortcuts to files:

- **History**. Contains shortcuts for all files you've used recently. This corresponds roughly to the Recently Used Documents list on the Windows Start menu.

- **My Documents**. The default folder for storing Access databases. Use this button to jump back there from some other folder you might have been browsing.

- **Desktop**. The folder that contains all the shortcuts on your Windows desktop. (You would seldom store a file there.)

- **Favorites**. A folder that contains shortcuts to all the files you've indicated you wanted there. You can add a shortcut to the Favorites folder by opening the **Tools** menu in the Save As or Open dialog box and choosing **Add to Favorites**.

- **Web Folders**. A folder that contains shortcuts to all your Web folders.

FINDING A DATABASE FILE

If you're having trouble locating your file, Access can help you look. Follow these steps to find a file:

1. Choose **File, Open** if the Open dialog box isn't already open.

2. (Optional) If you know part of the name, use wild cards to indicate it.

Wild Cards   You can use wild cards if you don't know the entire name of a file. The asterisk (*) wild-card character stands in for any character or set of characters, and the question mark (?) wild-card character stands in for any single character. For example, if you know the file begins with P, you can type **P*.mdb** to find all Access files that begin with P.

3. (Optional) If you want to look for a certain type of file, choose the type from the **Files of type** drop-down list.

4. Click the **Tools** button to open its menu, and choose **Find**. The Find dialog box appears (see Figure 6.5).

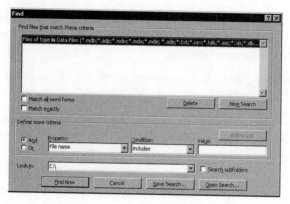

FIGURE 6.5   Use the Find dialog box to select the folders and drives you want to search.

5. In the Look In section at the bottom of the Find dialog box, narrow the search area as much as possible by using these techniques:

   • If you are sure the file is in a certain folder, type that folder's path (such as **C:\WINDOWS**) in the **Look in** box.

   • If you are sure the file is on a certain drive, select that drive from the **Look in** drop-down list.

   • If you don't know which drive contains the file, select **My Computer** from the **Look in** drop-down list.

6. Make sure that the **Search subfolders** check box is marked. If it isn't, click it.

7. If you want to specify any other properties, do so like this:

   a. Open the **Property** drop-down list and select a property, such as **File name** or **Creation date**.

   b. Open the **Condition** drop-down list and choose a condition. Your choices vary depending on the property you chose in step a.

c. Type a value to match in the **Value** text box. It must be appropriate for the property selected. For example, to find a file containing the name John Smith, type **John Smith**.

d. Click the **Add to List** button. The search string you just created appears at the top of the list in the Find Files that match these criteria box.

8. Click the **Find Now** button. The File Open dialog box reappears and displays the files that match your search criteria, if any are found.

9. Double-click the desired file to open it.

In this lesson, you learned how to save, close, and open a database. In the next lesson, you will learn how to create a table by using the Table Wizard.

LESSON 7

CREATING A TABLE WITH THE TABLE WIZARD

In this lesson, you will learn how to create a table by using the Table Wizard. To learn how to create a table from scratch, see Lesson 8.

WHY CREATE A TABLE?

Tables are the basis for the whole database. Tables hold your data; everything else is just dress up. If you created an empty database in Lesson 5, you'll need to create tables now, following the plan you developed in Lesson 2. If you used a database wizard to create your tables, you can create new tables here to augment them, or you can skip to Lesson 9, where you'll learn to modify and customize the tables.

When you create a table, you can create it "from scratch" or you can use the Table Wizard. This lesson covers the Table Wizard; Lesson 8 covers the less-automated method.

The Table Wizard can save you lots of time by creating and formatting all the right fields for a certain purpose. Access comes with dozens of pre-made business and personal tables from which to choose. You can pick and choose among all the fields in all the pre-made tables, constructing a table that's right for your needs. Even if you can't find all the fields you need in pre-made tables, you might want to use the Table Wizard to save time, and then add the missing fields later (see Lesson 9).

How Can I Know Beforehand? You won't know exactly what pre-made fields Access offers until you start the Table Wizard and review the listings. If you find that no tables meet your needs, you can click Cancel at any time and start creating your own table (see Lesson 8).

CREATING A TABLE USING THE TABLE WIZARD

If the fields you want to create are similar to any of Access's dozens of pre-made ones, the Table Wizard can save you a lot of time and effort. With the Table Wizard, you can copy fields from any of the dozens of sample tables.

To create a table using the Table Wizard, follow these steps:

1. In the database window, click the Tables object and then double-click **Create table by using wizard.**

 Other Methods Rather than follow step 1, you can open the New Table dialog box (by either clicking the New button in the database window or choosing Insert, Table). Then in the New Table dialog box, you can choose Table Wizard and click OK.

2. On the first Table Wizard dialog box (see Figure 7.1), click either **Business** or **Personal.** This determines the list of sample tables that will appear.

3. Choose a table from the **Sample Tables** list; its fields appear in the Sample Fields list.

4. Look at the **Sample Fields** list. If you see a field that you want to include in your new table, select it and then click the > button

to move it to the **Fields in my new table** list. To move the entire contents of the selected sample table to your list, click the >> button.

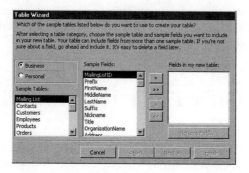

FIGURE 7.1   Choose your table's fields from those that come with any of the pre-made tables.

Name Change!   If you see a field that's close to what you want but you prefer a different name for it, first add it to your list (see steps 3 and 4). Then click the field name to select it; click the **Rename Field** button, type a new name, and click **OK**. This renames the field on your list only, not on the original.

5. Repeat steps 3 and 4 to select more fields from more sample tables until the list of fields in your new table is complete. You can remove a field from the list by clicking the < button. (You can also remove all the fields and start over by clicking the << button.) When you're finished adding fields, click **Next** to continue.

6. You're asked for a name for the table. Type a more descriptive name to replace the default one.

7. Click **Yes, set a primary key for me** to have the wizard choose your primary key field, or **No, I'll set the primary key** to do it yourself. (If you choose Yes, skip to step 10.)

Primary Key The designated field for which every record must have a unique entry. This is usually an ID number because most other fields could conceivably be the same for more than one record (for instance, two people might have the same first name).

8. The wizard next asks which field will be the primary key (see Figure 7.2). Open the drop-down list and select the field.

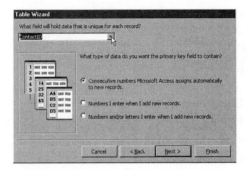

FIGURE 7.2   You can set your own primary key for the table.

9. Choose a data type for the primary key field:

- **Consecutive numbers Microsoft Access assigns automatically to new records.** Choose this if your primary key field is a simple record number—that is, if you want Access to number the records you enter consecutively as you enter them.

- **Numbers I enter when I add new records.** Pick this to enter your own numbers (Access won't let you enter any letters). This choice works well for unique ID numbers such as drivers' licenses.

- **Numbers and/or letters I enter when I add new records.** Pick this if you want to include both numbers and letters in the field. For instance, if your primary key field is a vehicle identification number for the cars in your fleet, you will need to enter both numbers and letters.

10. Click **Next** to continue.

11. If you already have at least one table in this database, a screen appears offering to create relationships between tables. Just click **Next** to move past it for now; you'll learn about relationships in Lesson 10.

12. At the Finish screen, click one of the following options:

   - **Modify the table design.** This takes you into Table Design view, the same as if you had created all those fields yourself. Choose this if you have some changes you want to make to the table before you use it.

   - **Enter data directly into the table.** This takes you to Table Datasheet view, where you can enter records into the rows of the table. Choose this if the table's design seems perfect to you as is.

   - **Enter data into the table using a form the wizard creates for me.** This jumps you ahead a bit in this book; it leads you right into the Form Wizard covered in Lesson 14. Leave this one alone for now if you want to continue following along with the lessons in this book in order.

13. Click **Finish** to move where you indicated you wanted to go in Step 12.

If you decide you don't want to work with this table anymore right now (no matter what you selected in step 12), just click the Close (✕) button for the window that appears.

Now you have a table. In the database window, when you click the Tables tab, you can see your table on the list. Figure 7.3 shows two tables.

These are not tables;
they are shortcuts to
performing actions.   Tables

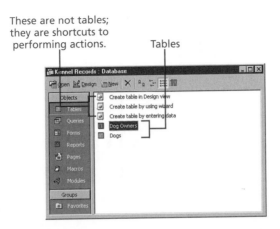

FIGURE 7.3   Now you have at least one table on your Tables tab.

NOW WHAT?

From here, you can go to a number of places:

- To learn how to create a table from scratch, continue on to Lesson 8, "Creating a Table Without a Wizard."

- To modify the table you just created, jump to Lesson 9, "Modifying a Table."

- To create relationships between tables, see Lesson 10, "Creating Relationships Between Tables."

- To enter data into your table, skip to Lesson 12, "Entering Data into a Table."

- To create a data entry form for easier data entry, check out Lesson 15, "Creating a Simple Form." (Don't do this yet if there are still modifications you'd like to make to your table.)

In this lesson, you learned to create a new table by using the Table Wizard. In the next lesson, you will learn how to create a table without the wizard.

LESSON 8

CREATING A TABLE WITHOUT A WIZARD

In this lesson, you will learn how to create a table in Table Design view.

WHY *NOT* USE A WIZARD?

Access's wizards are very useful, but they don't offer as much flexibility as performing the equivalent tasks "from scratch." For instance, if you want to create a table that contains special fields not available in a wizard, you are better off creating that table in Table Design view. You learn how in this lesson.

CREATING A TABLE IN TABLE DESIGN VIEW

To create a table in Table Design view, follow these steps:

1. In the Database window, double-click **Create table in Design view**. Table Design view opens (see Figure 8.1).

 Other Methods Instead of step 1, you can choose **Insert, Table** or click the **New** button in the database window to open the New Table dialog box. Then click **Design View** and then **OK**.

Start typing the first field name here.

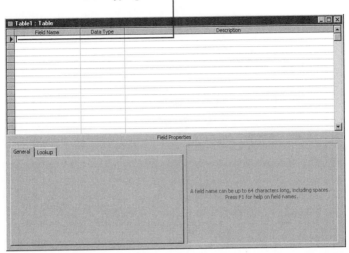

FIGURE 8.1   From Table Design view, you can control the entire table creation process.

3. Type a field name on the first empty line of the Field Name column. Then press **Tab** to move to the Data Type column.

4. When you move to the Data Type column, an arrow appears for a drop-down list there. Open the **Data Type** drop-down list and select a field type. (If you don't make a choice, the field will be a text field by default.) See the section "Understanding Data Types and Formats" later in this lesson if you need help deciding which field type to use.

Field Naming Rules   Field names in Access can be up to 64 characters long and can contain spaces if you like, and any symbols except periods (.), exclamation marks (!), accent grave symbols (`), or square brackets ([]). You might want to stick with short, easy-to-remember names, however. It's also advisable to avoid punctuation marks (such as $, %, or #) in field names, because some of them have special meanings in Access code.

5. Press **Tab** to move to the Description column, and type a description of the field. (This is optional; the table will work fine without it.)

6. In the bottom half of the dialog box, you see Field Properties for the field type you selected (see Figure 8.2). Make any changes to them that you want. See "Understanding Data Types and Formats" later in this lesson for help.

Field properties

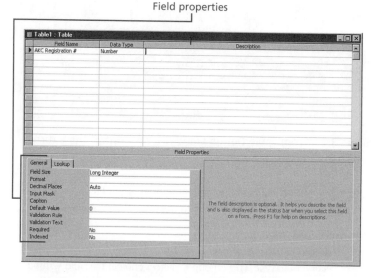

FIGURE 8.2   Field Properties change depending on the field type.

7. If you have more fields to enter, repeat steps 3 through 6.

8. Click the Table Design window's Close (×) button.

9. When you're asked if you want to save your changes to the table, click **Yes**. The Save As dialog box appears.

10. Type a name for the table in the **Table Name** text box, and then click **OK**.

Switching Between Views   At any time after you enter the first field, you can switch to Datasheet view to see how your table will look. Just select View, Datasheet, or click the Datasheet View button on the toolbar. You might be asked to save your work before you enter Datasheet view; if so, click Yes, enter a name, and then click OK.

No Primary Key!   When you close Table Design view, you might get a message that no primary key has been assigned. See the "Setting the Primary Key" section later in this lesson to learn about this.

UNDERSTANDING DATA TYPES AND FORMATS

Each field must have a type, so Access will know how to handle its contents. Here are the types you can choose from:

Text	Plain, ordinary typing, which can include numbers, letters, and symbols. A Text field can contain up to 255 characters.
Memo	More plain, ordinary text, except you don't set a maximum field length, so you can type an almost infinite amount of text (64,000 characters).
Number	A plain, ordinary number (not currency or a date). Access won't allow any text.
Date/Time	Simply a date or a time.

continues

continued

Currency	A number formatted as an amount of money.
AutoNumber	Access automatically fills in a consecutive number for each record.
Yes/No	The answer to a true/false question. It can contain one of two values: Yes or No, True or False, On or Off.
OLE Object	A link to another database or file. This is an advanced feature that this book doesn't cover.
Hyperlink	A link to a location on the Web. (See Lesson 27 for more information.)
Lookup Wizard	Lets you create a list to choose a value from another table or list of values in a combo box for each record. It's an advanced feature that you'll learn more about in Lesson 16.

In addition to a field type, each field has formatting options you can set. They appear in the bottom half of the dialog box, in the Field Properties area. The formatting options change depending on the field type; there are too many to list here, but following are some of the most important ones you'll encounter:

Field Size	The maximum number of characters a user can input in that field (applies only to Text fields).
Format	A drop-down list of the available formats for that field type. You can also create custom formats.
Decimal Places	For number fields, you can set the default number of decimal places a number will show.

Default Value	If a field is usually going to contain a certain value (for instance, a certain ZIP code for almost everyone), you can enter it here to save time. It will always appear in a new record, and you can type over it in the rare instances when it doesn't apply.
Required	Choose Yes or No to tell Access whether a user should be allowed to leave this field blank when entering a new record.

SETTING THE PRIMARY KEY

Almost every table should have at least one field that has a unique value for each record. For instance, in a table of the dogs your kennel owns, you might assign an ID number to each dog, and have an ID # field in your table. Or you might choose to use each dog's AKC (American Kennel Club) registration number. This unique identifier field is known as the *primary key field*. If the table is to be the "one" side of a one-too-many relationship, it is required to have a primary key. Otherwise, it is optional (but usually advisable).

 Primary Key Field   The designated field for which every record must have a unique entry. This is usually an ID number because most other fields could conceivably be the same for more than one record (for instance, two people might have the same first name).

You must tell Access which field you're going to use as the primary key, so it can prevent you from accidentally entering the same value for more than one record in that field. To set a primary key, follow these steps:

1. In Table Design view, select the field that you want for the primary key.

2. Select **Edit, Primary Key**, or click the **Primary Key** button on the toolbar. A key symbol appears to the left of the field name, as shown in Figure 8.3.

Key symbol

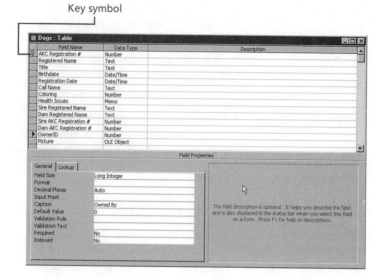

FIGURE 8.3   The primary key field is marked by a key symbol.

SWITCHING BETWEEN DESIGN AND DATASHEET VIEWS

When you're working with tables, two views are available: Design and Datasheet. One easy way to switch between the views is by clicking the down arrow next to the **View** button on the toolbar (see Figure 8.4). Then select the view you want from the drop-down list that appears.

FIGURE 8.4   Choose the view you want from the View button's drop-down list.

Another way to switch between views is as follows:

1. Open the **View** menu.

2. Select **Table Design** or **Datasheet**, depending on which view you're now in.

3. If you're moving from **Table Design** to **Datasheet** view, you might be asked to save your work. If so, click **Yes**.

4. If you're asked for a name for the table, type one and click **OK**.

CREATING A TABLE BY ENTERING DATA

Some people prefer to create their table in Datasheet view, but Microsoft designed Access's Datasheet view for data entry and viewing, not for table structure changes. I don't recommend creating the table this way, because you don't have access to as many design features as you do with Table Design view.

To create a table in Datasheet view, follow these steps:

1. In the database window, double-click **Create table by entering data**. A blank table opens (see Figure 8.5).

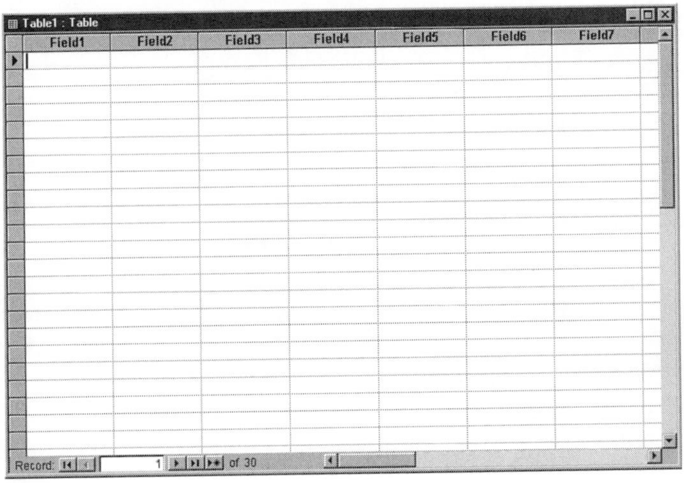

Figure 8.5 Creating a new table in Datasheet view gives you a quick, generic table.

2. Name the fields. When you create a table in Datasheet view, the fields have generic names such as Field1. To change a field name, click the present name to select the column. Then double-click the column name, type the new name and press **Enter**. Alternatively, you can select **Format**, **Rename Column**; or right-click the column name and choose **Rename column** from the shortcut menu, and then type the new name and press **Enter**.

3. Make any other changes to the design of the table (as explained in Lesson 9, "Modifying a Table").

4. Close the table by clicking its Close (×) button.

5. Access asks if you want to save the design changes. Click **Yes**.

6. Access asks for a name for the table. Type one and click **OK**.

In this lesson, you learned to create a table without the help of a wizard. Before you enter data into your table, you should make sure that it's exactly the way you want it. In the next lesson, you will learn how to make any changes needed to your table.

LESSON 9

MODIFYING A TABLE

In this lesson, you will learn how to change your table by adding and removing fields and hiding columns.

EDITING FIELDS AND THEIR PROPERTIES

Now that you've created a table, you might be eager to begin entering records into it. You'll learn to do that in Lesson 11. Before you begin, make certain that your table is structured exactly as you want it, so you don't have to backtrack later. You also might want to work through Lesson 10, "Creating Relationships Between Tables," before you start your data entry.

No matter how you created your table (either with or without the Table Wizard), you can modify it by using Table Design view. If you created the table without the Table Wizard, Table Design view will look very familiar to you.

To enter Table Design view, do one of the following:

- From the Database window, click the **Table** object type, select the table you want to work with, and click the **Design** button.

- From the Database window, click the **Table** object type, select the table you want to work with, and press **Alt+D**.

- If the table appears in Datasheet view, select **View, Design View**.

- From the Database window, right-click the table name and select **Design View** from the shortcut menu.

Don't forget that you can quickly change views with the **View** button at the far left end of the standard toolbar. (Refer to Figure 8.4 in the preceding lesson.) Click the down arrow next to the button, and select a view from the list that appears.

When you're in Table Design view (see Figure 9.1), you can edit any field, as you learned in Lesson 8. Here is the general procedure:

1. Click any field name in the **Field Name** column.

2. If desired, click the field's **Data Type** area and select a new data type from the drop-down list.

3. In the **Field Properties** pane (the bottom half of the Table Design window), click any text box to change its value. Some text boxes have drop-down lists, which you can activate by clicking in the box.

4. Repeat steps 1 through 3 for each field you want to change.

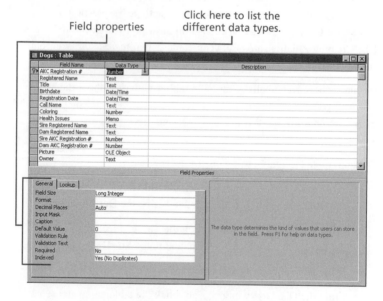

FIGURE 9.1   In Table Design view, you can modify the attributes of any field.

I Need More Help!   If you created your table without a wizard (Lesson 8), the preceding steps will be self-explanatory. However, if you used the Table Wizard, you might be lost right now. Review Lesson 8 to get up to speed.

ADDING FIELDS

Before you enter data into your table (see Lesson 11), you should make very sure that you have included all the fields you'll need. Why? Because if you add a field later, you might have to go back and enter a value in that field for each record that you already entered. Also, if you change the field length, you risk truncating or invalidating data that's already been entered.

You can add a field in either Table Design or Datasheet view. Try it in Table Design view first because you're already there:

1. Click the record selector (the gray square to the left of the field name) to select the field before which you want the new field to appear (the entire row is now highlighted in black).

2. Press the **Insert** button on the keyboard, click the **Insert Rows** button on the toolbar, or select **Insert, Row.** A blank row appears in the Field Name list.

3. Enter a name, type, description, and so on for the new field. (Refer back to Lesson 8 as needed.)

DELETING FIELDS

If you realize that you don't need one or more fields that you created, now is the time to get rid of them. Otherwise, you'll needlessly enter information into each record that you will never use.

Don't Remove Important Fields! Be very careful about deleting fields after you start entering records in your table. When you delete a field, all the information stored for each record in that field is gone too. The best time to experiment with deleting fields is now, before you enter any records.

You can remove fields from a table in either Table Design or Datasheet view. To delete a field in Table Design view, follow these steps:

1. Switch to Table Design view if you're not already there.

2. Select a field.

3. Do any of the following:

   • Press the **Delete** key on your keyboard.

   • Click the **Delete Rows** button on the toolbar.

   • Select **Edit, Delete Rows**.

The Delete Key Won't Work You can't delete a table column (field) in Datasheet view by using the **Delete** key—you must use the menu selection.

If you prefer, you can delete the field in Datasheet view. Unlike adding fields, where there's an advantage to using Table Design view, you can accomplish a field deletion easily in either view, and in Datasheet view you can see the data already entered into the field. Follow these steps to delete a field in Datasheet view.

1. Switch to Datasheet view if you're not already there.

2. Click the column heading to select the entire column for the field you want to delete (the entire column is now highlighted in black).

3. Select **Edit, Delete Column**.

HIDING A FIELD

If you don't want to use a field at the moment but will want to later, you might want to hide rather than delete it. Hiding a field has two advantages:

- If you've entered any records, you can preserve any data you entered into that field.

- The Field Properties you set when you created the field will remain intact, so you don't have to re-enter them later.

You must hide a field by using Datasheet view; you can't hide it using Table Design view. Follow these steps:

1. Switch to Datasheet view, if you aren't there already.

2. Select the field(s) you want to hide.

3. Select **Format**, **Hide Columns**, or right-click the column and select **Hide Columns**. The columns disappear.

To unhide the column(s) later, follow these steps:

1. Select **Format**, **Unhide Columns**. The Unhide Columns dialog box appears (see Figure 9.2). Fields with a check mark beside them are unhidden; fields without a check mark are hidden.

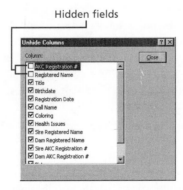

FIGURE **9.2**   You can unhide or hide fields with the Unhide Columns dialog box.

2. Click the check box of any field that you want to change. Clicking the box switches between hidden and unhidden status.

3. Click **Close**.

Hidden fields are still very much a part of your database. As proof of that, you'll still see them in Table Design view, along with all other fields.

DELETING A TABLE

Now that you've created a table and worked with it a bit, you might discover that you made so many mistakes in creating it that it would be easier to start over. (Don't feel bad; that's what happened to me the first time.) Or you might have several tables by now and find that you don't need all of them. Whatever the reason, it's easy to delete a table. Follow these steps:

1. From the database window, click the **Tables** object type.

2. Select the table you want to delete.

3. Select **Edit**, **Delete**, or press the **Delete** key on your keyboard.

4. A message appears asking whether you're sure you want to do this. Click **Yes**.

 Cut versus Delete   You can also *cut* a table. Cutting is different from deleting, because the table isn't gone forever; it moves to the Clipboard. From there, you can paste it into a different database or into some other application. The new Office 2000 multi-clipboard lets you save up to 12 separate items to paste into other applications.

In this lesson, you learned how to modify your table by adding and removing fields, hiding fields, and editing the information about each field. In the next lesson, you will begin learning about relationships between tables.

LESSON 10

CREATING RELATIONSHIPS BETWEEN TABLES

In this lesson, you will learn how to link two or more tables so that you can work with them much as you would a single table.

WHY CREATE RELATIONSHIPS?

Lesson 2 encourages you to make separate tables for information that's not directly related. When you create forms, queries, and reports, you can pull information from more than one table easily. But this works best when an appropriate relationship has been defined between the tables.

Suppose that I had two tables containing information about my customers. One table, Customers, contained their names and addresses; the other, Orders, contained their orders. The two tables would have a common field: Customer ID. All records in the Orders table would correspond to a record in the Customers table. (This is called a "one-to-many" relationship because there could be many orders for one customer.)

As another example, in my kennel database, I have several tables describing my dogs and their activities. I have a table listing all the different colorings a dog can have. I could create a relationship between the Dogs table and the Dog Coloring table, matching up each dog's coloring field with one of the accepted colors listed in the Dog Coloring table. This would ensure that I didn't record any dog's coloring as a type that's not allowed.

More Complicated I'm showing you only simple examples in this lesson. For more information on relationships, see your Access documentation or *Using Microsoft Access 2000*, published by Que Corporation.

CREATING A RELATIONSHIP BETWEEN TABLES

To create a relationship between tables, open the Relationships window and add relationships there. Follow these steps:

1. In the database, select **Tools, Relationships**, or click the **Relationships** button on the toolbar to open the Relationships window.

2. If you haven't selected any tables yet, the Show Table dialog box appears automatically (see Figure 10.1). If it doesn't appear, choose **Relationships, Show Table**, or click the **Show Table** toolbar button.

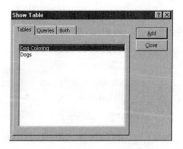

FIGURE 10.1 Add tables to your Relationships window with this dialog box.

3. Click a table that you want to use for a relationship, and then click the **Add** button.

4. Repeat step 3 to select all the tables you want, and then click **Close**. Each table appears in its own box on the Relationships window, as shown in Figure 10.2.

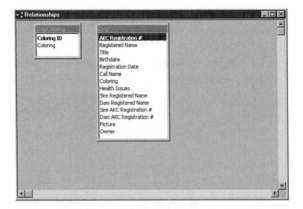

FIGURE 10.2   I've added two tables to my Relationships window for this example.

Make It Bigger   If you can't clearly see all the fields in a table's list, drag the table border to make it large enough to see everything. I've done that in Figure 10.2 to make the Dogs table completely visible.

5. Click a field in one table that you want to link to another table. For instance, I'm going to link the Coloring field in my Dogs table to the Coloring ID field in my Dog Coloring table, so I'll click the Coloring field in the Dogs table.

Field Type Matters   The fields to be linked must be of the same data type (date, number, text, and so on). The only exception is that you can link a field with an AutoNumber format to another field with a number format; AutoNumber fields are considered Long Integer number fields.

6. Hold down the mouse button and drag away from the selected field. Your mouse pointer turns into a little rectangle. Drop the little rectangle onto the destination field. For instance, I'm

dragging to the Color ID field in the Coloring table. The Edit
Relationships dialog box appears (see Figure 10.3).

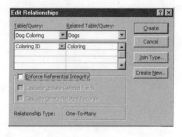

FIGURE 10.3 The Relationships dialog box asks you to define the relationship you're creating.

Matching Field Names Although it's not required, you will find it easier to match up linking fields if you give them the same name in both tables.

7. Choose any referential integrity options (see the following section), and then click **Create**. A relationship will be created, and you'll see a line between the two fields in the Relationships window (see Figure 10.4).

You won't see the ∞ and the 1 symbols if you didn't enforce referential integrity.

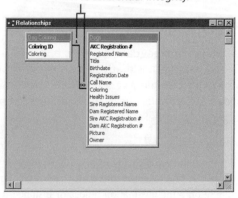

FIGURE 10.4 The line represents a relationship between the two fields.

Relationship Symbols   In Figure 10.4, notice that next to the Dogs table there's an infinity sign (∞), and next to the Dog Coloring table there's a 1. These symbols appear in relationships where **Enforce Referential Integrity** is turned on. The infinity sign means *many*—meaning many records in this table can match a single record (hence the 1 sign) in the related Dog Coloring table.

Multitable Forms   In Lesson 16, you learn how to use simple tables, like the Dog Coloring one shown in this lesson, to create a list from which users can select when entering records into a form.

WHAT IS REFERENTIAL INTEGRITY?

Referential integrity keeps you from making data-entry mistakes. It says, essentially, that all the information in the two fields should match.

For example, in the Coloring field in my Dogs database, I have a number that matches the Color ID field in the Dog Coloring table. The Coloring table lists all the allowable colors for the breed of dog. I don't want my employees to be able to accidentally enter a number in the Dogs table that doesn't match any of the colors in the Coloring table, so I chose to **Enforce Referential Integrity**. Now Access won't let anyone enter anything in the Coloring field of the Dogs table (the "many" or infinity side) except one of the numbers contained in the Color ID field in the Coloring table (the 1 side).

What happens if someone tries? It depends on which of the other two check boxes shown in Figure 10.3 were marked.

Here is a summary of what happens with the check boxes:

- **Cascade Update Related Fields marked.** If this check box is marked, and you make a change to the related table (in our example, the Dog Coloring table), the change will be made in the other table too (the Dogs table). For instance, if I decided to change a certain coloring number from 7 to 8, and I made the change in the Dog Coloring table (the 1 side), all the 7s in the Dog table (the many side) would change to 8s.

- **Cascade Delete Related Fields marked.** If this check box is marked, and you make a change to the 1 table (for instance, Dog Coloring) so that the entries in the related table aren't valid anymore, Access will delete the entries in the related table. For instance, if I deleted the record in the Dog Coloring table for Coloring ID number 3, all the dogs from my Dogs table that had coloring number 3 would also be deleted. (I would probably NOT want that!)

- **Neither check box marked.** Access gives an error message that you need a related record in the "[Table Name]" and won't let you make the entry.

The best time to set up referential integrity is before you enter any data in the tables. If you're following the lessons of the book in numerical order, you haven't entered data yet (you'll do that in Chapter 11), so you're all set.

If you try to create a relationship with referential integrity after you've already entered some data in one or both of the tables, you might see an error message the first time you try. For example, perhaps one of the fields uses a data type of Text while the other uses Number. (It wouldn't matter that you had entered only numbers in the field with the Text data type.) Read whatever error message appears carefully, and troubleshoot by making changes to the table design (as explained in Lesson 9).

EDITING A RELATIONSHIP

When a relationship is created, you can edit it by redisplaying the Relationships window (refer to Figure 10.2). To do so, double-click the relationship's line. From there, you can edit the relationship by using the same controls as you did when you created it.

REMOVING A RELATIONSHIP

To delete a relationship, just click it in the Relationships window (the line between the tables turn bold to indicate selection), and then press **Delete**. Access will ask for confirmation; click Yes, and the relationship disappears.

NOW WHAT?

Now that you've set up relationships between tables, how do you take advantage of them? To understand that answer, you need some more background knowledge. First, you need to learn how to enter and edit data in a table, and how to set up single-table versions of forms, queries, and reports. Only then will you be ready, in Lesson 25, to create the powerful multi-table forms, queries, and reports that are possible because of the relationships you have created.

This lesson shows you how to create, edit, and delete relationships between tables. In the next lesson, you will learn how to enter data into a table.

LESSON 11
ENTERING DATA INTO A TABLE

In this lesson, you will learn how to add records to a table, print the table, and close it.

ENTERING A RECORD

By now, you've created your table structure and fine-tuned it with the settings you want. It's finally time to enter records! So open the table and start.

> **Other Ways to Enter Records** Entering records directly into a table, which you learn how to do in this lesson, isn't always the best way to enter records. If you have many records to enter, it's often more efficient in the long run to take the time to create a form in which to do your data entry. You learn how to create a form in Lesson 14, "Creating a Simple Form."

If you read Lessons 1 and 2 (and I hope you did), you know that a record is a row in your table. It contains information about a specific person, place, event, or whatever. You enter a value for each record into each field (column) in your table.

First, you must open the table. Remember, to open a table, you double-click it in the Database window, or click it once and then click Open. Then follow these steps to enter a record.

There's a Number in the First Column!   If you've set up the first field to be automatically entered (for instance, a sequentially numbered field with AutoNumber), start with the second field instead.

1. Click the first empty cell in the first empty column.

 Plain English   Cell   The intersection of a row and a column. It's where you enter the data for a field for a particular record. Sometimes, the word *field* is used to mean the entry in a field for an individual record, but *field* really refers to the entire column. *Cell* is the proper name for an individual block.

2. Type the value for that field.

3. Press Tab to move to the next field and type its value.

4. Continue pressing Tab until you get to the last field. When you press Tab in the last field, the insertion point moves to the first field in the next line, where you can start a new record.

 Insertion Point   When you click a field, you see a blinking vertical line, called an *insertion point*, which tells you that's where anything you type will appear.

5. Continue entering records until you've entered them all.

SOME DATA-ENTRY TRICKS

You can enter all your data with nothing more than the Tab key and some typing, but here are a few keyboard tricks that make the job easier:

- To insert the current date, press Ctrl+; (semicolon). To insert the current time, press Ctrl+: (colon).

- To repeat the value from the same field in the previous record, press Ctrl+' (apostrophe).

MOVING AROUND IN A TABLE

In the earlier steps, you pressed Tab to move from field to field in the table, but you might find other ways to move around that are even more convenient. For instance, you can click in any field at any time to move the insertion point there. Table 11.1 summarizes the many keyboard shortcuts for moving around in a table.

TABLE 11.1 TABLE MOVEMENT KEYS

TO MOVE TO...	PRESS
Next field	Tab
Previous field	Shift+Tab
Last field in the record	End
First field in the record	Home
Same field in the next record	↓
Same field in the previous record	↑
Same field in the last record	Ctrl+↓
Same field in the first record	Ctrl+↑
Last field in the last record	Ctrl+End
First field in the first record	Ctrl+Home

PRINTING A TABLE

Normally, you won't want to print a table—it won't look very pretty. A table is just a plain grid of rows and columns. Instead, you'll want to create and print a report that contains exactly the data you want (see Lesson 23, "Creating a Simple Report").

Sometimes, however, you might want a quick printout of the raw data in the table. In that case, follow these steps:

1. Open the table (by double-clicking it or choosing it and clicking **Open**).

2. Click the **Print** button on the toolbar. The table prints.

 More Printing Control   You can set some printing options before you print if you want. Rather than click the Print toolbar button, choose **Print** from the **File** menu and select your printing options from the Print dialog box. Then click **OK** to print.

CLOSING A TABLE

By now you've probably discovered that a table is just another window; to close it you simply click its Close button (×), press **Ctrl+F4**, or double-click its Control-menu icon (see Figure 11.1).

Control-menu icon   Close button

FIGURE 11.1   Close a table the same way you would close any window.

In this lesson, you learned to enter records into a table, to print the table, and to close it. In the next lesson, you will learn how to edit your table data.

LESSON 12

EDITING DATA IN A TABLE

In this lesson, you will learn how to change information in a field, select records, and insert and delete records.

CHANGING A CELL'S CONTENT

Very few things are done perfectly the first time around. As you enter records into your table, you might find you need to make some changes. Editing a cell's content is easy. You can replace the old content completely or edit it. Which is better? It depends on how much you need to change—you make the call.

REPLACING A CELL'S CONTENT

If the old content is completely wrong, it's best to enter new data from scratch. To replace the old content in a field, follow these steps:

1. Select the cell by moving to it with the keyboard (see Table 11.1 in Lesson 11) or by clicking it. (If you tab to the new cell, the entire contents are selected automatically.)

   To select the cell by clicking it, position the mouse pointer at the left edge of the field so the mouse pointer becomes a plus sign (see Figure 12.1); then click once. That way you select the entire content.

2. Type the new data. The new data replaces the old data.

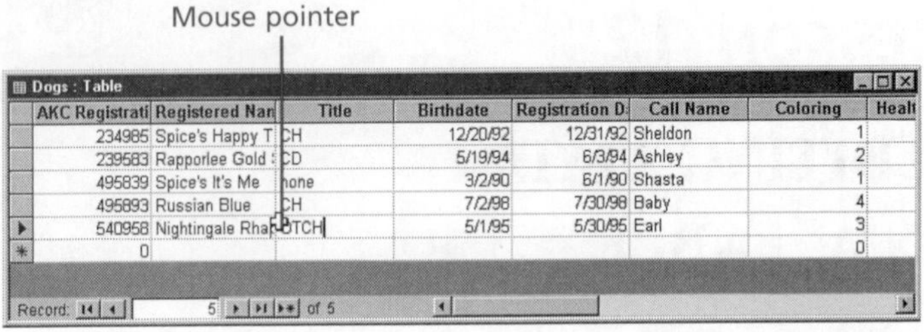

Mouse pointer

FIGURE 12.1 To select a field's entire content, make sure that the mouse pointer is a plus sign when you click.

EDITING A CELL'S CONTENT

If you have a small change to make to a cell's content, there's no reason to completely retype it; just edit the content. Follow these steps:

1. Position the mouse pointer in the cell, so the mouse pointer looks like an I-beam.

2. Click once. An insertion point appears in the cell (see Figure 12.2).

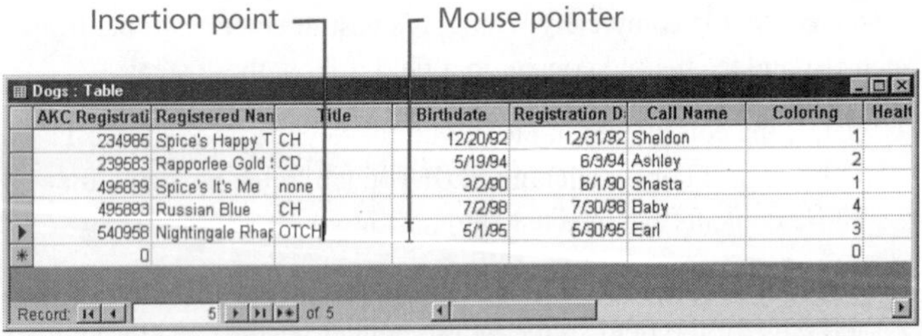

Insertion point —┐   ┌— Mouse pointer

Figure 12.2   Click inside the cell to place the insertion point in it.

3. Move to the location in the cell where you want to start editing (see Table 12.1).

4. Press Backspace to remove the character to the left of the insertion point, or Delete to remove the character to the right of it. Then type your change.

TABLE 12.1   MOVING AROUND WITHIN A CELL

TO MOVE	PRESS
One character to the right	$\rightarrow$
One character to the left	$\leftarrow$
One word to the right	Ctrl+$\rightarrow$
One word to the left	Ctrl+$\leftarrow$
To the end of the line	End
To the end of the cell	Ctrl+End
To the beginning of the line	Home
To the beginning of the cell	Ctrl+Home

SELECTING RECORDS

In addition to editing individual cells in a record, you might want to work with an entire record. To do this, click the gray square to the left of the record (the record selector). The entire record appears highlighted (white letters on black), as shown in Figure 12.3.

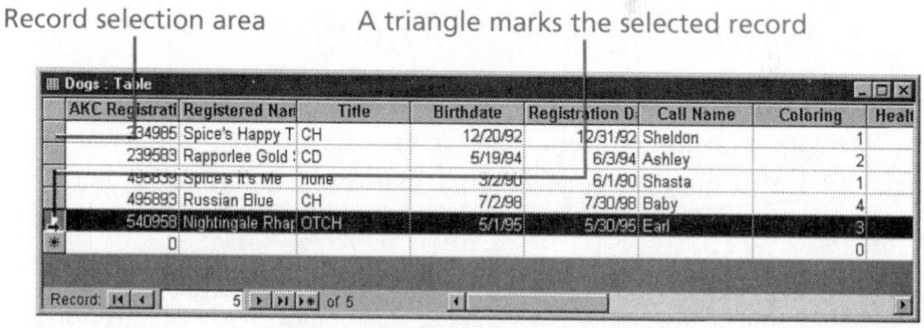

Record selection area   A triangle marks the selected record

Figure 12.3   The highlighted selected record.

You can select several records as a group (select the first one and hold down Shift while you select the others). You can select only contiguous groups of records; you can't pick them from all over the list.

Selecting All Records   You can select all records at once in several ways. Click the blank box at the inter-section of the row and column headings; press Ctrl+A; or choose **Select All Records** from the **Edit** menu.

UNDERSTANDING RECORD SELECTION SYMBOLS

When you select a record, a triangle appears in the record selection area (refer to Figure 12.3). You might see two other symbols in this area, too:

              Being entered or edited

              Empty line for next new record

 Only One Triangle   If you select several records, only the first one you click will have the triangle symbol beside it. That doesn't matter, though; they're all equally selected.

INSERTING NEW RECORDS

New records are inserted automatically. When you start to type a record, a new line appears below it, waiting for another record, as you can see in Figure 12.3. You can't insert new records between existing ones; you must always insert new records at the end of the table.

 What If I Want the Records in a Different Order?   It's easy to sort your records in any order you want. You learn how to sort in Lesson 19, "Sorting, Indexing, and Filtering Data."

DELETING RECORDS

If you find that one or more records is out-of-date or doesn't belong in the table, you can easily delete it. You can even delete several records at a time. Follow these steps:

1. Select the record(s) you want to delete.

2. Do any of the following:

    • Click the Delete Records button on the toolbar.

    • Press the Delete key on the keyboard.

    • Choose **Delete** from the **Edit** menu.

    • Choose **Delete Record** from the **Edit** menu.

    • Right-click the record(s) and choose **Delete Record**.

 Delete versus Delete Record   If you select the entire record, there's no difference between these two commands. If you don't select the entire record, though, Delete removes only the selected text, whereas Delete Record removes the entire record. You can't undo a deletion, so be careful what you delete.

MOVING AND COPYING DATA

As with any Windows program, you can use the Cut, Copy, and Paste commands to copy and move data. Follow these steps:

1. Select the field(s), record(s), cell(s), or text that you want to move or copy.

2. Do any of the following:

    • Open the **Edit** menu and select **Cut** (to move) or **Copy** (to copy).

    • Click the Cut or Copy button on the toolbar.

- Right-click the record(s) and choose Cut or Copy from the shortcut menu.

- Press **Ctrl+X** to cut or **Ctrl+C** to copy.

3. Position the insertion point where you want to insert the cut or copied material.

4. Do any of the following:

- Choose **Paste** from the **Edit** menu.

- Click the Paste button on the toolbar.

- Press **Ctrl+V** to paste.

- Right-click where you want it to go, and choose Paste from the shortcut menu.

 Moving and Copying Entire Tables   You can move and copy entire objects, not just individual fields and records. From the Database window, select the table, report, query, and so on, that you want to move or copy; then use the Cut or Copy command. Move where you want the table to go (for example, in a different database) and execute the Paste command.

In this lesson, you learned to edit data in a field, insert and delete fields, and copy and move data from place to place. In the next lesson, you will learn about table formatting.

Lesson 13

Formatting a Table

In this lesson, you will learn how to improve the look of a table by adjusting the row and column sizes, changing the font, and choosing a different alignment.

Why Format a Table?

Most people don't spend a lot of time formatting Access tables simply because they don't have to look at or print their tables. They use data-entry forms (see Lesson 14, "Creating a Simple Form") to see the records onscreen, and reports (see Lesson 23, "Creating a Simple Report") to print their records. The tables are merely holding tanks for raw data.

However, creating forms and reports might be more work than you want to tackle right now. For instance, if your database is very simple, consisting of one small table, you might want to add enough formatting to your table to make it look fairly attractive; then you can use it for all your viewing and printing, foregoing the fancier forms and reports.

Even if you decide later to use a form or report, you might still want to add a bit of formatting to your table, so it will be readable if you ever need to look at it.

Changing Column Width and Row Height

One common problem with a table is that you can't see the complete contents of the fields. Fields often hold more data than will fit across a column's width, so the data in your table appears *truncated*, or cut off.

You can fix this problem in two ways: make the column wider, so it can display more data, or make the row taller, so it can display more than one line of data.

CHANGING COLUMN WIDTH

Access offers many different ways to adjust column width in a table, so you can choose the method you like best. One of the easiest ways to adjust column width is to simply drag the column headings. Follow these steps:

1. Position the mouse pointer between two field names (column headings), so the mouse pointer turns into a vertical line with left- and right-pointing arrows (see Figure 13.1). You'll be adjusting the column on the left; the column on the right will move to accommodate it.

Mouse pointer

	AKC Registrati	Registered Nam	Title	Birthdate	Registration D	Call Name	Coloring	Healt
	234985	Spice's Happy T	CH	12/20/92	12/31/92	Sheldon	1	
	239583	Rapporlee Gold	CD	5/19/94	6/3/94	Ashley	2	
	495839	Spice's It's Me	none	3/2/90	6/1/90	Shasta	1	
	495893	Russian Blue	CH	7/2/98	7/30/98	Baby	4	
▶	540958	Nightingale Rhap	OTCH	5/1/95	5/30/95	Earl	3	
*	0						0	

Record: 14 ◀ | 5 ▶ ▶I ▶* of 5

FIGURE 13.1   Position the mouse pointer between two column headings.

2. Click and hold the mouse button and drag the edge of the column to the right or left to increase or decrease the width.

3. Release the mouse button when the column is the desired width.

Alternatively, you can double-click the column's vertical line when the double-headed arrow is showing to automatically adjust the width of the column on the left so its data just fits.

Another, more precise way to adjust column width is to use the Column Width dialog box. Follow these steps:

1. Select the column(s) you want to adjust the width for.

2. From the **Format** menu choose **Column Width**, or right-click and choose Column Width from the shortcut menu. The Column Width dialog box appears (see Figure 13.2).

FIGURE **13.2**   Adjust column width precisely here.

3. Do one of the following to set the column width:

   • Adjust the column to exactly the width needed for the longest entry in it by clicking **Best Fit**.

   • Set the width to a precise number of field characters by typing a value in the **Column Width** text box.

   • Reset the column width to its default value by selecting the **Standard Width** check box.

4. Click **OK** to apply the changes.

CHANGING ROW HEIGHT

If you don't want to make a column wider but still want to see more of its contents, you can make the rows taller.

Which Rows Should I Adjust?   It doesn't matter which row you've selected; the height you set applies to all rows. You can't adjust the height of individual rows.

One way to make rows taller is to drag one, just as you dragged a column in the preceding section. Position the mouse pointer between two rows in the row selection area; then drag up or down.

Another way is with the Row Height dialog box. It works the same as the
Column Width dialog box, except that there's no Best Fit option. Right-
click the column, select **Row Height,** and then enter a new height.
Alternatively, from the **Format** menu choose **Row Height,** enter the new
height, and click **OK.**

CHANGING THE FONT

Unlike other Access objects (such as Report and Form), you can't format
individual table fields or entries to be different from the rest. You can
choose a different font for the display, but it automatically applies to all
the text in the table, including the column headings.

Font changes you make in Datasheet view won't appear in your reports,
queries, or forms; they're for Datasheet view only.

 Why Would I Change the Datasheet Font?   You
might want to make the font smaller so you can see
more of the field contents onscreen without bother-
ing to adjust column width. Or you might make the
font larger so you can see the table more clearly. You
can change the default font used in Datasheet view
by choosing **Tools, Options** and making the change on
the dialog box's Datasheet page.

To choose a different font for the table datasheet, follow these steps:

1. From the **Format** menu choose **Font.** The Font dialog box
   appears (see Figure 13.3).

2. Select a font from the **Font** list box.

3. Select a style from the **Font style** list box.

4. Select a size from the **Size** list box.

5. Select a color from the **Color** drop-down list.

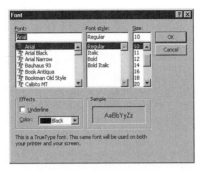

FIGURE 13.3   The Font dialog box lets you set one font for the entire table.

6. (Optional) Click the **Underline** check box if you want underlined text.

7. You can see a sample of your changes in the Sample area. When you're happy with the look of the sample text, click **OK**.

More Cell Appearance Changes   Another way you can change the look of your table is with the Datasheet Formatting dialog box (choose **Format, Datasheet**). You can change the cell special effect, background color, the color of the grid lines between each row and column, and whether the lines show.

In this lesson, you learned how to format a table. In the next lesson, you will learn how to create a simple data-entry form.

LESSON 14

CREATING A SIMPLE FORM

In this lesson, you will learn how to create a form, with and without the Form Wizard.

WHY CREATE FORMS?

As you saw in Lessons 11 and 12, you can do all your data entry and editing in a table, but that might not be the best way. For one thing, unless you set your column widths very wide (see Lesson 13), you probably can't see everything you type in a field. Also, if you have data you want to enter into several tables, you must open each table individually.

A better data-entry method is to create a form. With a form, you can allot as much space as needed for each field, and you can enter information into several tables at once. You can also avoid the headaches that occur when you try to figure out which record you're working with on a table; generally, each form shows only one record at a time.

There are three ways to create a form:

- AutoForms provide very quick, generic forms that contain all the fields in a single table.

- The Form Wizard helps you create a form by following a series of dialog boxes and choosing the fields and style for the form

- Creating a form from scratch provides a layout grid on which you place fields. It's the more difficult way, but it provides the most control.

CREATING A FORM WITH AUTOFORM

The easiest way to create a form is with AutoForm. AutoForm simply plunks the fields from a single table into a form; it's the least flexible way but it's very convenient. Follow these steps

1. From the Database window, click the **Forms** object type.

2. Click the **New** button. The New Form dialog box appears (see Figure 14.1).

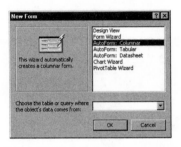

FIGURE 14.1   Choose how you want to create your form.

3. Click **AutoForm: Columnar** to create a columnar form (the most popular kind). This creates a form that contains your fields in a single column, from top to bottom. Or click **AutoForm: Tabular** for a form that resembles a table, or **AutoForm: Datasheet** for a form that resembles a datasheet.

4. Open the drop-down list at the bottom of the dialog box and choose the table or query to use as the source of the form's data.

5. Click **OK**. The form appears, ready for data entry.

The form you get with an AutoForm might not be very pretty. The field labels might be cut off, and the fields might be too close together to be attractive. If the form created by AutoForm isn't what you want, delete it and try again with the Form Wizard. To delete the form, close it, and answer **No** when asked if you want to save your changes.

CREATING A FORM WITH FORM WIZARD

The Form Wizard offers a good compromise between the automation of AutoForm and the control of creating a form from scratch. Follow these steps to use the Form Wizard:

1. From the Database window, click the **Forms** object type.

2. Double-click **Create form by using wizard**. The Form Wizard opens (see Figure 14.2).

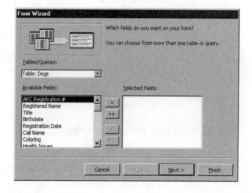

FIGURE **14.2**   The Form Wizard lets you choose which fields you want to include, from as many different tables as you like.

3. From the **Tables/Queries** drop-down list, choose a table or query from which to select fields. (By default, the first table in alphabetical order is selected, which probably isn't what you want.)

4. Click a field in the **Available Fields** list that you want to include on the form, and then click the > button to move it to the **Selected Fields** list.

5. Repeat step 4 until you've selected all the fields you want to include from that table. If you want to include fields from another table or query, go back to step 3 and choose another table.

Selecting All Fields   You can quickly move all the fields from the Available Fields list to the Selected Fields list by clicking the >> button. If you make a mistake, you can remove a field from the Selected Fields list by clicking it and clicking the < button.

6. Click Next to continue. You're asked to choose a layout: Columnar, Tabular, Datasheet, or Justified. Click each button to see a preview of that type (Columnar is the most common). Then click the one you want and click Next.

7. You're asked to choose a style. Click each style listed to see a preview of it; click Next when you've chosen the one you want.

8. Enter a title for the form in the text box at the top of the dialog box.

9. Click the Finish button. The form appears, ready for data entry (see Figure 14.3).

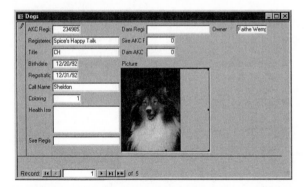

FIGURE 14.3   The Form Wizard has created this rough but usable form. The first record in the table appears in it.

If your form's field labels are cut off, like the ones in Figure 14.3, you should edit the form to move the fields over so there's more room. You learn how to move fields around to improve the look in Lesson 15.

CREATING A FORM FROM SCRATCH

The most powerful and difficult way to create a form is with Form Design view. In this view, you decide exactly where to place each field and how to format it.

 Don't Use the Shortcut Now   You might be tempted to double-click the **Create form in Design view** shortcut in the Forms list, but if you go this route, rather than the route outlined in the following steps, you won't have the opportunity to select a table. You can select the table later from the form's RecordSource property, but that's rather advanced. It's best to stick with the steps here, if you're a beginner.

The following steps introduce you to Form Design view; you'll learn more about this view in Lesson 15.

1. From the Database window, click the Forms object type.

2. Click the New button. The New Form dialog box appears. (You saw this back in Figure 14.1.)

3. Click **Design View**.

4. Select a table or query from the drop-down list at the bottom of the dialog box. (You can change the table later on, if you need to, from the RecordSource property in the form's properties sheet.)

5. Click **OK**. A Form Design window appears (see Figure 14.4). You're ready to create your form.

In the next lesson, you'll learn to
create other areas besides Detail.

Field List

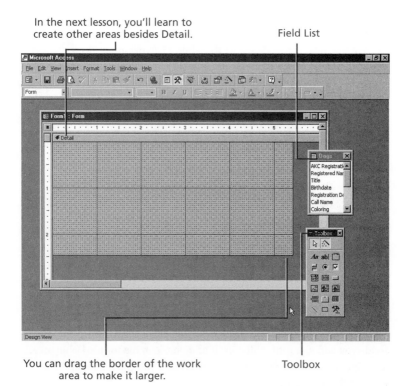

You can drag the border of the work
area to make it larger.

Toolbox

FIGURE 14.4 Form Design view presents a blank canvas on which to design your form.

  Adding Another Table to the Form If you later need to add another table to the form's data source, click the **Build** button (...) to the right of the RecordSource property to open the Query Designer. In the Query Designer, you can add a new table to the upper pane and, if necessary, set up a relationship to the original table. After closing the Query Designer, you should see the fields from both tables in the field list.

Toolbox and Field List   You'll want to use the Form
Design toolbox and the Field List shown in Figure
14.4. If they're not visible, click the Toolbox button or
the Field List button in the toolbar.

ADDING CONTROLS TO A FORM

 Controls and Fields   When you are working with a
table, you work directly with *fields* of data; on forms
and reports you work with *controls*, which are elements that display data from a field, informative text
(such as titles and labels), or are purely decorative
(such as lines and rectangles).

The basic idea of the Form Design window is simple: it's similar to a light
table or paste-up board where you place the elements of your form. The
fields you add to a form will appear as controls in the form's Detail area.
The Detail area is the only area visible at first; you'll learn to add other
areas in the next lesson.

To add a control displaying a field to the form, follow these steps:

1. Display the Field List if it's not showing. Click the Field List
    button or choose Field List from the View menu to do so.

2. Drag a field from the Field List onto the Detail area of the form
    (see Figure 14.5), where it will appear as a text box control.

3. Repeat step 2 to add as many fields as you like to the form.

Don't worry about crowded labels; you'll fix that in the next lesson.

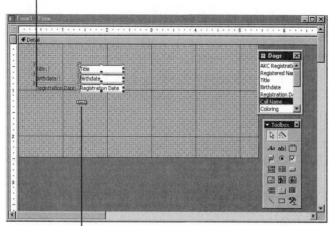

The mouse pointer changes to show a field is being placed.

FIGURE 14.5   Drag fields from the Field List to the grid.

When you drag a field to a form from the Field List, it becomes a control that displays data from that field. You can drag more than one field to the form at once. In step 2, rather than click and drag a single field, do one of the following before dragging:

- To select a block of fields, click the first one you want and hold down Shift while you click the last one.

- To select non-adjacent fields, hold down Ctrl as you click each one you want.

- To select all the fields on the list, double-click the **Field List** title bar.

You can move objects around on a form after you initially place them; you'll learn how to do this in the next lesson. Don't worry if your form doesn't look very professional at this point; in the next several lessons, you see how to modify and improve your form.

Using Snap to Grid   If you find it hard to align the fields neatly, choose **Snap to Grid** from the **Format** menu to place a check mark next to that command. If you want to align the fields on your own, select it again to turn it off.

If you are satisfied with your form, go ahead and close it by clicking its Close (×) button. When asked if you want to save your changes, choose **Yes**. Type a name for the form in the text box provided, and then click **OK**. If, on the other hand, you want to make more modifications to your form, leave it open and skip to Lesson 15 now.

ENTERING DATA IN A FORM

The point of creating a form is so that you can enter data more easily into your tables. The form acts as an attractive "mask" that shields you from the plainness of your table. When you create a form, follow these steps to enter data into it:

1. Open the form:

   - If your form appears in Form Design view, choose **View, Form View** to enter Form view or select **Form View** from the **View** button.

   - If the form isn't open at all, click the **Form** tab in the Database window and then double-click the form's name or click the **Open** button.

2. Click the field you want to begin with and type your data.

3. Press Tab to move to the next field. If you need to go back, you can press **Shift+Tab** to move to the previous field. When you reach the last field, pressing Tab moves you to the first field in a new, blank record.

To move to the next record before you reach the bottom field or to move back to previous records, click the right and left arrow buttons on the left end of the navigation bar at the bottom of the window.

4. Repeat steps 2 and 3 to enter all the records you like. They're saved automatically as you enter them.

Data-Entry Shortcuts   See the "Some Data-Entry Tricks" section in Lesson 11 for some shortcut ideas. They work equally well in forms and tables.

In this lesson, you created a simple form and added data to it. In the next lesson, you will learn how to make changes to your form to better suit your needs.

Lesson 15
Modifying a Form

In this lesson, you will learn to modify a form. You can use any form, created in any of the ways you learned in Lesson 14.

Cleaning Up Your Form: An Overview

The form you have onscreen now (from Lesson 14) might be functional, but it's probably not attractive. In this lesson, you learn how to make it look better. Here's an overview picture of what you need to do to make a more attractive form:

1. Move the controls as needed to create more space between them. See the next section, "Moving Controls."

2. Adjust the spacing between each control and its label. See "Moving Controls and Their Labels Independently."

3. Resize any controls or labels needed so they aren't truncated. See "Resizing Controls."

4. Add any explanatory text needed. See "Adding Text."

5. Add form headers and footers if needed. See "Viewing Headers and Footers."

6. Add text formatting to the text on your form (for example, make the text in labels bold or a different font, or make the form header label text large). See "Formatting Controls."

MOVING CONTROLS

The most common change to a form is to move a control around. You might want to move several controls down so you can insert a new control, or you might want to just rearrange how the controls appear.

 More Space   If you want to create extra space at the bottom of the controls so that you have more room to move them around, drag the Form Footer pane down, so more of the Detail area is visible. You can also drag the right side of the grid to make the form wider. If you need more space at the top of the form, highlight all the controls and move them down as a group.

Follow these steps:

1. If you aren't already in Form Design view, enter it, as you learned in Lesson 14.

2. Click a control's name to select it. Selection handles appear around it. You can select several controls by holding down Shift as you click each one.

3. Position the mouse pointer so the pointer becomes a hand (see Figure 15.1). If you're moving more than one control, you can position the mouse pointer on any selected control.

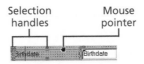

Selection   Mouse
handles   pointer

FIGURE 15.1   To move a control, first select it. Then drag it when the mouse pointer is a hand shape.

4. Click and hold down the left mouse button as you drag the control to a different location.

5. Release the mouse button when the control is at the desired new location. You can stretch a control vertically or horizontally from any side, or diagonally from any corner.

The Label Moved Without the Text Box Attached!
Be careful when you position the mouse pointer over the control to be moved. Make sure that the pointer changes to an open hand, as shown in Figure 15.1. If you see a pointing finger, move elsewhere. The pointing finger is used to move controls and labels independently, as you'll learn in the following section.

You can move many controls at once, maintaining their relative positions, by selecting all the controls first and then dragging. To select multiple controls, click each one you want while holding down the Ctrl key. Or use the mouse to drag an outline around all the controls you want to select.

MOVING CONTROLS AND THEIR LABELS INDEPENDENTLY

Sometimes you might need to move a text box control or a field label independently of the other. For example, you might want to make a field's label box longer, so that the field name displayed in its caption doesn't appear cut off. (The next section shows how to change a control's length.) But to do that, you must first move the text box control to the right, to make room for a longer label.

To move a text box or its attached label by itself, follow these steps:

1. Click the control that you want to move.

2. Position the mouse pointer over the selection handle at the top left, so that it becomes a pointing finger (see Figure 15.2).

 Text Boxes: The Most Commonly Used Controls   Text boxes and their attached labels are discussed in this lesson, but the same methods can be used with other controls that may have attached labels, such as combo boxes and images.

3. Drag the control to a new position.

FIGURE **15.2**   Drag with a pointing hand mouse cursor to move the control or label independently.

  Deleting Labels   If a certain control is self-explanatory (such as a picture), you might want to delete its attached label. To do so, select the label and press Delete.

RESIZING CONTROLS

After you adjust the spacing between each text box and its label as needed (as in the preceding section), follow these steps to change a controlís length:

1. Click the control to select it. Selection handles appear around it.

2. Position the mouse pointer at the right edge, so the pointer turns into a double-headed arrow (see Figure 15.3).

3. Drag the control to its new length, and then release the mouse button.

Mouse pointer

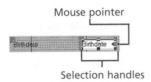

Selection handles

FIGURE **15.3**   You can change the size of the control entry area by dragging it.

Multiline Labels   If the text displayed in a text box or label control is too long to fit in the allotted space, consider making it multiline by dragging its bottom selection handle down. That way, its text can wrap to the next line, so it doesn't require so much space from side to side.

VIEWING HEADERS AND FOOTERS

You've been working with the Detail area so far, but you can use other areas:

- *Form Header and Form Footer.* A place for text that should be repeated at the top or bottom of the form, such as a form title at the top or a copyright notice at the bottom.

- *Page Header and Page Footer (rarely used).* A place for text that should be repeated at the top or bottom of every page of the form when you print the form. These aren't displayed by default; to display bars for them, choose **View, Page Header/Footer**.

When you create a form with the Form Wizard, the Form header and Form Footer bars appear in Design view, but there's nothing in them. And the Form Header bar is butted up against the Detail bar, so the header area has no height.

To make some room to work in the Form Header (see Figure 15.4), click the Form header bar to select it, position the mouse pointer between the bars (the cursor changes to a double-headed arrow), and drag down.

The Detail section contains
controls whose data
changes with every record.

The Form Header contains
text you want repeated
on each onscreen form.

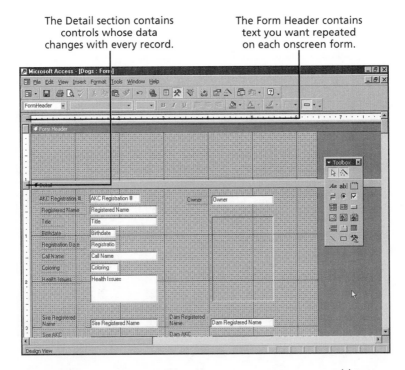

FIGURE 15.4   Drag the Detail bar down to create space to add text in the header.

After you display a header or footer, you can add controls to these sections.

ADDING LABELS

The next thing that most people want to do is add text to the form, in the form of label controls to display titles, subtitles, explanatory text, and so on. Add titles and other general information to a header or footer; add information specific to particular controls to the Detail area. Follow these steps:

1. If the Toolbox isn't displayed, choose **Toolbox** from the **View** menu or click the Toolbox button on the toolbar.

2. Click the Label tool in the toolbox (the one with the italicized letters *Aa* on it). The mouse pointer changes to a capital A with a plus sign next to it (see Figure 15.5).

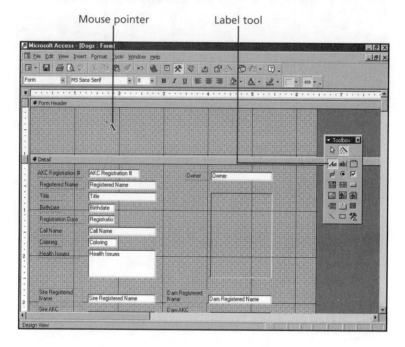

FIGURE 15.5   Select the Label tool in the toolbox.

3. Click anywhere on the form where you want to create the new text. A tiny box appears. (The box expands to hold the text as you type.)

4. Type the text.

You Must Type the Text Now! If you don't type anything before you go on to step 5, the box will disappear as soon as you click away from it.

5. Click anywhere outside the control's area to finish, or press Enter.

Label Dragging   Don't worry about positioning the label as you create it; you can move a label control in the same way that you move other controls. Just click it, position the mouse pointer so the hand appears, and then drag it to where you want it to go.

FORMATTING CONTROLS

After you place all your information on the form (that is, the controls you want to include and labels to display any titles or explanatory text), the next step is to make the form look more appealing.

All the formatting tools you need are on the Formatting toolbar (the second toolbar from the top in Form Design view). Table 15.1 shows the tools. To format a control, just select it, and then click the appropriate formatting tool to apply the format to the control.

 Control Properties   You can right-click any control and choose Properties from its shortcut menu to open a Properties box that contains fields that control all the formatting options and other settings for the control.

TABLE 15.1   TOOLS ON THE FORMATTING TOOLBAR

TOOL	PURPOSE
MS Sans Serif	Lists the available fonts
18	Lists the available sizes for the selected font
B	Toggles Bold on/off

continues

TABLE 15.1   CONTINUED

TOOL	PURPOSE
I	Toggles Italics on/off
U	Toggles Underline on/off
	Left-aligns text
	Centers text
	Right-aligns text
	Fills the selected box with the selected color
A	Colors the text in the selected box
	Colors the outline of the selected box
	Adds a border to the selected box
	Adds a special effect to the selected box

Some tools, like the font and size tools, are drop-down lists. You click the down arrow next to the tool, and then select from the list. Other tools are simple toggle buttons for turning bold and italic on or off. Still other tools, such as the coloring and border tools, combine a button and a drop-down list. If you click the button, it applies the current value. You can click the down arrow next to the button to change the value.

Changing the Background Color   You can change the color of the form background, too. Just click the header for the section you want to change (for instance, **Detail**) to select the entire section. Then right-click and choose **Fill/Back** color to change the background color.

AutoFormat   Here's a shortcut for formatting your form. Choose **Format, AutoFormat**. You're asked to choose from among several pre-made color and formatting schemes. If you don't like the formatting after you apply it, press Ctrl+Z to undo.

CHANGING TAB ORDER

When you enter data on a form, you press Tab to move from control to control in the order they're shown in the form. The progression from control to control is the *tab order*. When you first create a form, the tab order runs from top to bottom.

When you move and rearrange controls, the tab order doesn't change automatically. For instance, if you had 10 controls arranged in a column and you rearranged them so that the 10th one was at the beginning, the tab order would still show that control in 10th position, even though it's now at the top of the form. This makes it more difficult to fill in the form, so you'll want to adjust the tab order to reflect the new structure of the form.

Tab Order Improvements   You might want to change the tab order to be different from the obvious top-to-bottom structure, to make data entry easier. For instance, if 90 percent of the records you enter skip several controls, you might want to put those controls last in the tab order, so you can skip over them easily.

Follow these steps to adjust the tab order:

1. Choose **View, Tab Order,** or right-click the square in the form's upper-left corner and select **Tab Order** from the shortcut menu. The Tab Order dialog box appears (see Figure 15.6).

FIGURE 15.6   Use the Tab Order dialog box to decide what tab order will be used on your form.

2. Choose the section for which you want to set tab order. The default is **Detail**.

3. The controls appear in their current tab order. To change the order, click a control and then drag it up or down in the list.

4. To quickly set the tab order based on the controls' current positions in the form (top to bottom), click the **Auto Order** button.

5. Click **OK**.

Removing a Control from the Tab Order   If you want to completely remove a control from the Tab order, you can't delete it in the Tab Order dialog box, but you can remove it from the Tab order in the conrol's properties sheet. Select the control, click the Other tab in its properties sheet, and select No for its tab stop property. The control will still show up in the Tab Order dialog, but you won't be able to get to it by using the Tab key.

In this lesson, you learned to improve a form by moving controls, adding text, adding formatting, and adjusting the tab order. In the next lesson, you will learn about some of the fancier controls you can add to a form.

LESSON 16
CREATING SPECIAL DATA-ENTRY FIELDS ON A FORM

In this lesson, you will learn about some special controls you can include on your forms.

WHY USE SPECIAL DATA-ENTRY CONTROLS?

As you'll see in this lesson, it takes a little extra time to set up one of Access's special data-entry controls on a form. Here are some reasons why you should do it:

- Special data-entry controls make your form look more professional.

- They decrease the amount of typing you have to do when entering records.

- They decrease the possibility of typing errors, making for more reliable data.

Figure 16.1 shows the sample form you'll be working with in this lesson, with a list box, option group, and command buttons already created. You can see how these controls make the form much more attractive and easy to use!

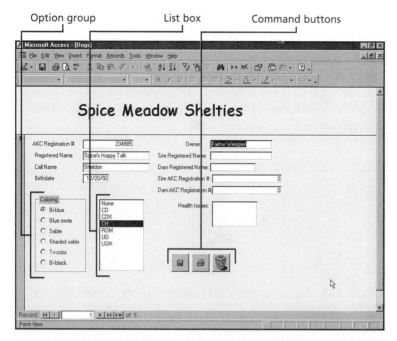

FIGURE 16.1   Special data-entry controls make the difference.

WHAT KINDS OF CONTROLS?

You can use several controls:

- *List box.* Presents a list from which you choose an item.

- *Combo group.* Like a list box, but you can type in other entries besides those on the list.

- *Option group.* Gives you options to choose from (but you can select only one). You can use option buttons, toggle buttons, or check boxes.

- *Command button.* Performs some function when you click it, such as starting another program, printing a report, saving the record, or anything else you specify.

- *Other controls.* In Access 2000, you can place ActiveX controls or any other kind of control or object on a form. For example, you can include a video clip for each record.

Access comes with a wizard for most of these control types, which makes it easy for you to use the controls.

For the benefit of advanced users, Access can create these controls with or without the wizards. To make sure that Access knows you want to use wizards, select the **Control Wizards** button in the Toolbox (see Figure 16.2). Because creating custom controls without a wizard is rather difficult, this lesson focuses on the wizards.

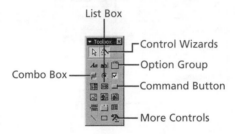

List Box

Combo Box

Control Wizards

Option Group

Command Button

More Controls

Figure 16.2   To use wizards, make sure that the Control Wizards button is selected.

CREATING A LIST BOX OR COMBO BOX

A list box or combo box can come in handy if you find yourself typing certain values repeatedly into a field. For example, if you have to enter the name of one of your 12 branch offices each time you use a form, you might find it easier to create a list box containing the branch office names, and then you can click to select from the list. With a list box, the person doing the data entry is limited to the pretyped choices that display.

A combo box is useful when a list box is appropriate, but it's possible that a different entry might occasionally be needed. For example, if most of your customers come from one of six states but occasionally you get a new customer from another state, you might use a combo box. During data entry, you could choose the state from the list when appropriate and type a new state when it's not.

Follow these steps to create a list box or combo box from Form Design view:

1. Make sure that the Control Wizards button in the toolbox is selected.

2. Click the List Box or Combo Box button in the toolbox (refer to Figure 16.2). The mouse pointer changes to show the type of box you selected.

3. Drag your mouse to draw a box on the grid where you want the new control to be. When you release the mouse button, the wizard starts.

4. In the wizard's first dialog box, click the button labeled **I will type in the values that I want.** Then click **Next.**

 Another Way to Enter Values   If you prefer, you can create a separate table beforehand containing the values you want to use in this field, and then select **I want the list box to look up the values in a table or query.** Then choose the table or query rather than type in the values.

5. You're asked to type in the values that you want to appear in the list. Type them in (as shown in Figure 16.3), pressing the Tab key after each one. Then click **Next.**

6. Select **Store that value in this field,** and choose which field should receive the data. For example, I'm entering the various titles a dog can earn in dog shows, so I'll select the Title field here and click **Next.**

7. Type the title that you want to appear for the control (that is, the text of its attached label).

8. Click **Finish.** Your new list box appears, bound to the field that you chose in step 6 in the box.

9. (Optional) If the list box is self-explanatory and doesn't require a label, select its label and press Delete to remove it.

One column is usu-
ally sufficient.

Drag here to change
the column width.

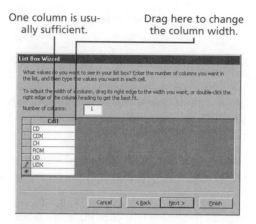

FIGURE 16.3   Type the values that you want to choose from in this list or combo box.

Where Are My Values?   Don't be alarmed that the values you entered for the field don't appear in the box. You'll see them in Form view, when you drop down the list. You can switch to Form view to see them now if you want to be sure; switch back to Form Design view after you finish looking.

I Picked the Wrong Type!   You can easily switch between a list box and a combo box, even after you create it. In Form Design view, right-click the control, click **Change to**, and select a new control type.

CREATING AN OPTION GROUP

An option group is helpful if you have a few choices for a field entry and never enter anything but those few choices. For instance, if you're recording the results of a multiple-choice quiz, the answer to question 5 is always A, B, C, or D—never anything else.

What About "Other" As a Quiz Answer?   If you have a questionnaire in which the respondent can choose A, B, C, or D, or enter his own response under Other, you're better off using a combo box on your form because a combo box allows for new entries.

An option group can include toggle buttons, option buttons, or check boxes. These are simply different styles; they all do the same thing. You can select only one choice shown in an option group. When you select another, the one you originally selected is deselected.

 Faking a Multi-Select Option Group   If you want the look of an option group where you can check several check boxes at once, you can make several standalone check boxes and enclose them a rectangle.

 That's Not How Check Boxes Usually Work!   You're right. In almost all Windows programs, check boxes are nonexclusive. You can select as many of them in a group as you like. But in this case, they aren't real check boxes; they're just option buttons that you can style to resemble check boxes or toggle buttons if you want.

To create an option group, follow these steps:

1. Make sure that the Control Wizards button in the toolbox is selected.

2. Click the Option Group button in the toolbox (refer to Figure 16.2). Your mouse pointer changes to show the Option Group icon.

3. Drag your mouse pointer on your form to draw a box where you want the option group to appear. When you release the mouse button, the wizard starts.

4. You're asked to enter the values you want for each button (see Figure 16.4). Do so, pressing Tab after each one; then click **Next**.

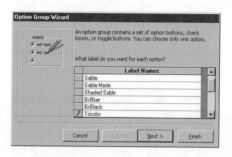

FIGURE **16.4**   Enter the labels you want for each option here.

5. Choose **Yes** or **No** when asked whether you want a default choice. If you choose **Yes**, select the default choice from the drop-down list (this choice appears automatically when you use the form). Then click **Next**.

6. When asked what value you want to assign to each option, click **Next** to continue. You don't need to change the assigned default values.

7. Click **Store the value in this field,** and choose which field should receive the data from the drop-down list. For instance, I'm entering the various colors a Shetland Sheepdog can be, so I'll select the Coloring field here and click **Next**.

8. Click to select a type of control (option button, check box, or toggle button) and a style for the controls; then click Next.

9. Enter a caption for the option group (for example, Coloring). Then click **Finish**. You've created your group.

They're All Marked!   When you're in Form Design view, each option in an option group is selected, just to show that it can be. When you're actually using the form, however (in Form view), only one option in the group can be selected at a time. If you don't select a default option (step 5), all of them will be gray (neither selected nor unselected) for a record until you choose one.

ADDING COMMAND BUTTONS

You're probably already familiar with command buttons. They're buttons, in dialog boxes and elsewhere, that you click to perform actions. For example, in Figure 16.1, the form has command buttons to **Save**, **Print**, and **Delete** the current record.

Access offers a wide variety of functions you can perform with command buttons:

- *Record navigation.* You can add command buttons that move users to the next, previous, first, or last record.

- *Record operations.* You can make buttons that delete, duplicate, print, save, or undo a record.

- *Form operations.* Command buttons can print a form, open a page (on a multipage form), close the form, and more.

- *Report operations.* Command buttons can print a report, send a report to a file, mail a report, or preview a report.

- *Application.* Command buttons can quit Access or run some other application.

- *Miscellaneous.* Command buttons can print a table, run a macro, run a query, or use the AutoDialer.

To place a command button on a form, follow these steps:

1. Make sure that the Control Wizards button in the toolbox is selected.

2. Click the Command Button button in the toolbox (refer to Figure 16.2). Your mouse pointer changes to show the Command Button icon.

3. Click your form where you want the command button to appear. The Command Button Wizard opens.

4. Select an action category, and then an action (see Figure 16.5). Then click Next.

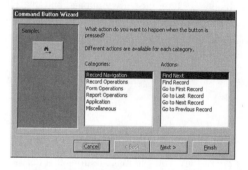

FIGURE 16.5   Choose what action you want the command button to execute.

5. Depending on your choice of action, there may be another screen of options to choose. Fill in the extra information if prompted, and then click Next.

6. Choose Text or Picture for the button's face. If you choose Text, enter the text you want; if you choose Picture, select a picture from the list. Then click Next.

7. Type a name for the button.

8. Click Finish. The button appears on your form. You can move it around as with any other control.

INSERTING ACTIVEX CONTROLS

ActiveX controls are new kinds of OLE controls used to share information among Office programs, or add extra functionality to your forms. Most beginning users have no occasion to use them, but you might occasionally need to employ one. If you have Office 2000 Developer, it includes a set of extra ActiveX controls that you can use with all Office programs.

To place an ActiveX control on a form, follow these steps:

1. From the **Insert** menu choose **ActiveX Control**. The Insert ActiveX Control dialog box opens.

2. Choose the type of control you want.

3. Click OK. The control appears on the form.

4. Drag it to the spot where you want it.

Then right-click it and choose Properties to set up its properties.

If the control that you want doesn't appear on the list in the preceding steps, try the More Controls list. Click the More Controls button in the Toolbox for a complete list of controls you can include on a form, including almost any kind of ActiveX control imaginable. Make your selection, and then click the form to place it.

 Why Doesn't My ActiveX Control Work?   Just because an ActiveX control appears in the list doesn't mean it will work in Access. Actually, only a small selection of ActiveX controls work in Access. If you insert one that doesn't work in Access, you will get a Registry not loaded message when you switch to Form view.

In this lesson, you learned to create list and combo boxes, option groups, command buttons, and other controls on your forms. In the next lesson, you will learn how to further improve the look of a form by adding graphics to it.

LESSON 17

ADDING GRAPHICS TO FORMS

In this lesson, you will learn how to improve the look of a form by adding graphics to it.

WHY ADD GRAPHICS TO FORMS?

It's not just an old cliche: A picture is worth a thousand words. Graphics do make a difference. Using clip art and other pictures and graphics on your Access form can make your form look more professional and polished.

You can include several kinds of graphics in a form. You can import a piece of clip art that comes with Microsoft Office and pictures from other programs (in a variety of formats). Or, by using the Windows Paint program, you can draw a picture yourself.

 Clip Art Predrawn "generic" images that you can put to use in your computerized databases, documents, spreadsheets, and so on. Clip art isn't copyrighted, so you can use it without paying royalties or getting permission.

IMPORTING CLIP ART

If you're used to other Microsoft Office programs, such as Word and PowerPoint, you might be disappointed to learn that Microsoft Access doesn't directly use the Clip Gallery program as the others do. However, if the Clip Gallery has been installed with another Office program, you can use it through Access. Follow these steps:

1. In Design view, select the section on the form where you want the picture to go (Form Header, Detail, or Form Footer).

2. Choose **Insert, Object** or click the Unbound Object tool in the Toolbox to insert an unbound object control on the form. The Insert Object dialog box opens.

3. Choose **Microsoft Clip Gallery** from the list of object types.

4. Click **OK**. The Clip Gallery window appears.

5. Click the category of clip you want (for example, **Animals** or **Business**). The available clips appear.

6. Click the clip art image you want, and then click its **Insert Clip** button (see Figure 17.1).

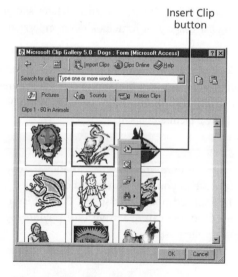

Insert Clip
button

Figure 17.1 Select a clip from the Clip Gallery.

7. Click **OK** to close the Clip Gallery.

8. Drag the clip around on the form to position it as needed.

If you need to resize the clip, see "Resizing a Graphic" later in this lesson.

IMPORTING A GRAPHIC

You can place any graphic on a form, not just clip art. To place a graphic from a file on a form, follow these steps:

1. Display the form in Form Design view.

2. Click inside the section in which you want to place the graphic (the Form Header or Detail area).

3. Choose **Insert, Picture**, or click the **Image** tool in the Toolbox to insert an Image control on the form. The Insert Picture dialog box appears (see Figure 17.2).

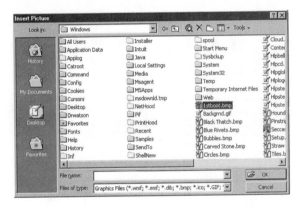

FIGURE 17.2   Choose the picture you want to import from this dialog box.

4. If you want to see only a certain file type on the list, open the **Files of type** drop-down list at the bottom of the dialog box, and select the file type you want. By default, Graphics Files appears there, which includes all types of graphics files on the list, including clip art, bitmap files (created with Windows Paint program), and more.

5. Change the drive or folder, if necessary, to locate the graphic file you want. (See Lesson 6, "Saving, Closing, and Opening a Database," if you need help navigating the drives and folders.)

6. (Optional) If you aren't sure which file you want, click the **Views** button in the dialog box until the Preview pane appears. The view changes to show the currently highlighted file (see Figure 17.3). Click various files on the list to preview them before you make your selection.

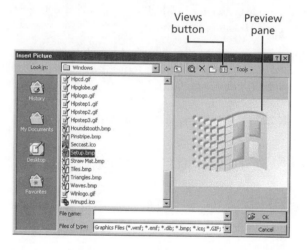

FIGURE 17.3   You can preview graphics before you import them.

7. When you've found the graphic you want to import, click **OK**. The graphic appears on your form.

8. Drag the graphic to the desired location.

RESIZING A GRAPHIC

To resize a graphic, drag one of its corner selection handles. If you don't want the picture to change shape as you drag, hold down the **Shift** key while dragging to maintain the aspect ratio (the ratio of height to width). If you don't hold down **Shift**, Access allows you to squash or elongate the picture as you resize.

If the picture crops itself, rather than shrinks or grows, when you try to resize it, follow these steps to change the image's properties so it can be resized:

1. Right-click the image and choose **Properties**. The object's property sheet appears.

2. On the Format page, click in the **Size Mode** property's field. It's probably set to **Clip**.

3. From the **Size Mode** drop-down list choose **Stretch** (see Figure 17.4).

4. Click the Close (×) button in the corner of the property sheet.

FIGURE **17.4**   Change the SIZE MODE to STRETCH if your image won't resize.

CREATING A NEW PICTURE

Another way to get a graphic onto your form is to draw it yourself. You can use the Windows Paint program to create a simple drawing without leaving Access.

Paint   A simple art program that comes with Windows 95/98 and Windows NT versions 3.51 and higher. You can use it to make simple drawings, but it's not sophisticated enough to create professional-quality artwork. Try a program such as CorelDRAW or Freehand if you need to create higher-quality art.

To use Paint, follow these steps:

1. Open the form in Form Design view.

2. Select **Insert, Object**. The Insert Object dialog box appears, with a Paint toolbox on the left and a color palette on the bottom.

3. In the **Object Type** list, choose **Bitmap Image**.

4. Click OK.

   A blank Paint screen appears embedded in your form, as shown in Figure 17.5.

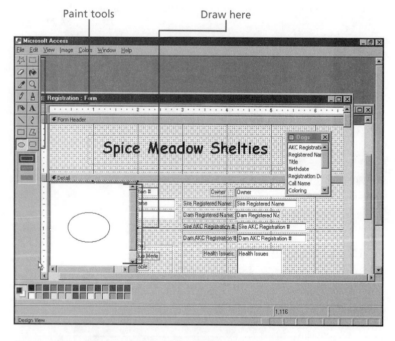

FIGURE 17.5   Use Paint to create a picture.

5. Use the paint tools (as described in your Windows documentation) to create your drawing.

6. Click your form outside the Paint drawing area. Paint closes and your form returns to normal.

7. If you want to edit the drawing, double-click it to re-enter Paint.

In this lesson, you learned how to import pictures into an Access form, and how to use Paint from within Access to create a picture. You'll see that these skills also apply to reports when you learn to create those in Lesson 23, "Creating a Simple Report." In the next lesson, you will learn how to search for data in an Access database.

LESSON 18

SEARCHING FOR DATA

In this lesson, you will learn the most basic ways to search for data in a database using the features in the Find and Replace dialog box.

USING THE FIND FEATURE

The Find feature is useful for locating a particular record that you have previously entered. For instance, if you keep a database of customers, you might want to find a particular customer's record quickly when he is ready to make a purchase, so you can verify his address. Or, to continue the kennel example I've been using, you could quickly find the record for the dog with the call name of Sheldon, to look up his birth date.

 Finding More Than One Record If you need to find several records at once, Find is not the best tool because it finds only one record at a time. A better tool for finding multiple records is a filter, discussed in Lesson 19, "Sorting, Indexing, and Filtering Data."

To find a particular record, follow these steps:

1. Look at your table in Datasheet view, or examine its content by using a form. Either view supports the Find feature.

2. Click in the field that contains the data you want to find, if you know which field it is.

3. Click the **Find** tool in the toolbar, select **Edit, Find,** or press **Ctrl+F**. The Find and Replace dialog box appears (see Figure 18.1) with the Find page on top.

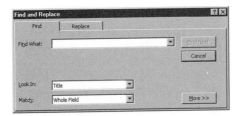

FIGURE 18.1   Use the Find and Replace dialog box to find data in a record.

4. Type the text or numbers that you want to find into the **Find What** text box.

5. The default value for **Look In** is the field you selected in step 2. If you want to search the entire table, drop down the **Look In** list and select the table's name.

6. From the **Match** drop-down list select one of the following:

   - **Whole Field** finds fields where the specified text is the only thing in that field. For instance, "Smith" would not find "Smithsonian."

   - **Start of Field** finds fields that begin with the specified text. For instance, "Smith" would find "Smith" and "Smithsonian," but not "Joe Smith."

   - **Any Part of Field** finds fields that contain the specified text in any way. "Smith" would find "Smith," "Smithsonian," and "Joe Smith."

7. If you want to specify a search direction, search for a particular capitalization, or match formatting, click the **More** button to access additional controls (see Figure 18.2). If not, skip to step 11.

8. If you want to search forward only from the current record, open the **Search** drop-down list and select **Down**. If you want to search backward only, select **Up**. The default is **All**, which searches all records.

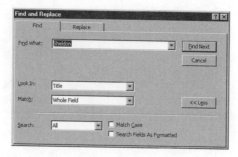

FIGURE 18.2 When you click **More**, these additional controls appear. Click **Less** to hide them again.

9. To limit the match to only entries that are the same case (upper or lower), select the **Match Case** check box. After doing this, "Smith" won't find "SMITH" or "smith."

10. To find only fields with the same number or date formatting as the text you type, select **Search Fields As Formatted**. With this option on, "12/12/95" won't find "12-12-95," even though they are the same date, because they're formatted differently.

Don't Slow Down Don't use the **Search Fields As Formatted** option unless you specifically need it because it makes your search go more slowly.

11. Click **Find Next** to find the first match for your search.

12. If needed, move the Find and Replace dialog box out of the way by dragging its title bar so that you can see the record it found. Access highlights the field entry containing the found text (see Figure 18.3).

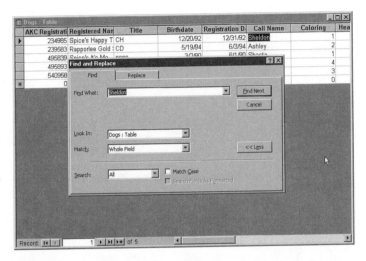

FIGURE 18.3 Access finds records that contain the selected text, one instance at a time.

13. To find the next occurrence, click **Find Next**. If Access can't find any more occurrences, it tells you the search item was not found. Click **OK** to clear that message.

14. When you finish finding your data, click **Cancel** to close the Find and Replace dialog box.

USING THE REPLACE FEATURE

Replacing is a lot like finding, except as an extra bonus, it replaces the found text with text that you specify. For instance, if you found that you misspelled a brand name in your inventory, you could replace the word with the correct spelling. Or, in our dog kennel example, you could find the dog named Sheldon and change his name to Sherman, if his new owners changed his name.

To find and replace data, follow these steps:

1. Select **Edit**, **Replace**, or press **Ctrl+H**. The Find and Replace dialog box appears with the Replace controls displayed (see Figure 18.4).

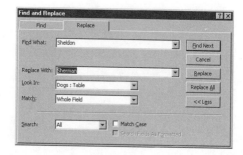

FIGURE 18.4   You can find specific text and replace it with different text.

 Find to Replace   If the Find and Replace dialog box is already open (from the preceding steps in this lesson), you can jump to the Replace controls by clicking the Replace tab.

2. Type the text you want to find in the **Find What** text box.

3. Type the text you want to replace it with in the **Replace With** text box.

4. Select any options you want, as you learned to do with the Find dialog box in the previous section.

5. Click **Find Next**. Access finds the first occurrence of the text.

6. If needed, drag the title bar of the Replace dialog box to move the box so you can see the text that was found.

7. Click the **Replace** button to replace the text.

8. Click **Find Next** to find other occurrences if desired, and replace them by clicking the **Replace** button.

Replace All   If you are certain you want to replace every instance of the text in the entire table, click **Replace All**. It's quicker than alternating repeatedly between **Find Next** and **Replace**. Be careful, though! You might not realize all the instances that might be changed—for instance, you wouldn't want to change "will" to "would" only to find that "willfully" has been changed to "wouldfully." Unlike Word's Find and Replace feature, there's no "Whole Word" option in the Access Find and Replace dialog box.

Caution   Unlike Word's Find and Replace, there is no "Whole Word" option in the Access Find and Replace dialog box.

9. When you finish replacing, click **Cancel**.

OTHER WAYS TO FIND DATA

The Find and Replace feature works well on individual records, but there are several more sophisticated ways of locating data in your database, as you'll learn in upcoming lessons. They include

- **Sorting**. Rearranging the data onscreen so that it's easier to skim through the list to find what you want. See Lesson 19, "Sorting, Indexing, and Filtering Data."

- **Filtering**. Narrowing down the list to eliminate the data you know you don't want to see. See Lesson 19.

- **Indexing**. Defining other fields besides the primary key that you want Access to keep track of (that is, keep an index of). Indexing is optional, but in large databases it makes your searching and sorting faster. See Lesson 19.

- **Querying**. Creating a more formal filter with complex criteria that you can save and apply again and again. See Lessons 20 through 22.

- **Reporting**. Creating a printed report containing only the records and fields that you're interested in. See Lessons 23 and 24.

In this lesson, you learned how to find and replace data in a database. In the next lesson, you will learn about other ways of locating the data you want: sorting, filtering, and indexing.

LESSON 19

SORTING, INDEXING, AND FILTERING DATA

In this lesson, you will learn how to find data by sorting and filtering and how to speed up searches with indexing.

FINDING AND ORGANIZING YOUR DATA

Access has many ways of finding and organizing data, and each is good for a certain situation. As you learned in Lesson 17, Find and Replace is very useful when you're working with individual instances of a particular value—for example, finding Mr. Smith's record quickly. This lesson explains other ways of finding what you need.

SORTING DATA

Even though you enter your records into the database in some sort of logical order, at some point you'll want them in a different order. For instance, if you entered the dogs in the kennel database according to registration number, you might later want to look at the list according to the dogs' birth dates, from oldest to youngest.

The Sort command is the perfect solution to this problem. With Sort, you can rearrange the records according to any field you like. You can sort in either ascending (A to Z, 1 to 10) or descending (Z to A, 10 to 1) order.

 Which View? You can sort in either Form or Datasheet view, but I prefer Datasheet view because it shows many records at once.

Follow these steps to sort records:

1. Click anywhere in the field on which you want to sort.

2. Click the **Sort Ascending** or **Sort Descending** button on the toolbar. Or, if you prefer, select **Records, Sort**, and then choose **Ascending** or **Descending**. Figure 19.1 shows the table of dogs sorted in Ascending order by birth date.

3. To restore the records to their presorted order, select **Records, Remove Filter/Sort**.

AKC Registrati	Registered Nar	Title	Birthdate	Registration D	Call Name	Coloring	He
234520	Wempen's Best	none	3/18/85	8/25/85	Buddy	2	
495839	Spice's It's Me	none	3/2/90	6/1/90	Shasta	1	
493029	Spice's Never M	CH	4/9/90	4/9/90	Cindy	4	
394821	Spice's Krazy 4	UDX	4/9/90	4/9/90	Betsy Mae	4	
493492	Princess of the F	None	8/12/91	9/2/91	Bubbles	3	
234985	Spice's Happy T	CH	12/20/92	12/31/92	Sheldon	1	
495092	Happiglade Torn	UD	2/3/94	4/5/94	Ruby	1	
409385	King of the Hill	CD	2/3/94	4/5/94	Champ	2	
239583	Rapporlee Gold	CD	5/19/94	6/3/94	Ashley	2	
540958	Nightingale Rhap	OTCH	5/1/95	5/30/95	Earl	3	
209483	Carrolton Make a	CD	9/12/95	9/12/95	Boopsie	1	
450981	Brazen Puppy G	None	3/3/96	5/6/96	Loudmouth	2	
495893	Russian Blue	CH	7/2/98	7/30/98	Baby	4	
0						0	

Record: 14 ◁ | 1 ▷ ▷1 ▷* of 13

FIGURE 19.1 Access sorted this table in Ascending order by the Birthdate column.

What Is Presorted Order? If you defined a primary key field when you created your database (see Lesson 7), the records appear sorted in ascending order according to that field by default. This is the order they revert to when you remove a sort (as in step 3). If you save the datasheet or form without removing the sort, the sort order becomes part of that object.

FILTERING DATA

Filtering is for those times when you want to get many of the records out of the way so that you can see the few that you're interested in. Filtering temporarily narrows down the number of records that appear, according to criteria you select.

 Filters versus Queries   Queries also narrow down the records displayed, as you'll learn in Lesson 20. A filter is easier and quicker to use than a query, but a filter can't be saved as a separate object for later use. (However, you can save a filter *as a query*, as you'll learn later in this lesson.)

You can apply a filter in three ways: Filter by Selection (or Filter Excluding Selection), Filter by Form, and Advanced Filter/Sort. The first two are the most common for casual users, so the following sections cover them. The third method is for advanced users only.

 Sorting and Filtering   Neither of the filtering methods you'll learn in this lesson allow you to sort at the same time that you filter. However, it's easy enough to sort the filtered records, using the same sorting process you learned earlier in this lesson.

FILTER BY SELECTION

Filtering by selection is the easiest method of filtering, but before you can use it, you have to locate an instance of the value you want the filtered records to contain. For example, if you want to find all the dogs in your table that have earned the title of CD (Companion Dog), you must first locate a record meeting that criteria. You'll base the rest of the filter on that record.

To filter by selection, follow these steps:

1. In a field, find one instance of the value that you want all filtered records to contain.

2. Select the value:

   • To find all records in which the field value is identical to the selected value, select the entire field entry.

   • To find all records in which the field begins with the selected value, select part of the field entry beginning with the first character.

   • To find all records in which the field contains the selected value at any point, select part of the field entry beginning after the first character.

3. Click the **Filter by Selection** button on the toolbar, or select **Records, Filter, Filter by Selection**. The records that match the criteria you selected appear.

Figure 19.2 shows the Dogs table filtered to show only dogs that have earned the CD title.

Access filtered the table
by this column.

AKC Registrati	Registered Name	Title	Birthdate	Registration D	Call Name	Coloring
239583	Rapporlee Gold Star	CD	5/19/94	6/3/94	Ashley	
409385	King of the Hill	CD	2/3/94	4/5/94	Champ	
209483	Carrolton Make a Wish	CD	9/12/95	9/12/95	Boopsie	
0						

Record: 1 of 3 (Filtered)

FIGURE **19.2**   The result of a filter; only the records that match the criteria appear.

Filtering by Multiple Criteria   With Filter by Selection, you can filter by only one criterion at a time. However, you can apply successive filters after the first one to further narrow the list of matching records.

You can also filter for records that *don't* contain the selected value. Follow the same steps as before, but choose **Records, Filter, Filter Excluding Selection** in step 3.

You can cancel a filter by clicking the **Toggle Filter** button, or by selecting **Records, Remove Filter/Sort**.

Filter by Form

Filtering by form is a more powerful filtering method than filtering by selection. With Filter by Form, you can filter by more than one criterion at a time. You can also set up "or" filters, which find records in which any one of several criteria is matched. You can even enter logical expressions (such as "greater than a certain value").

To filter by form, follow these steps:

1. In Datasheet or Form view, click the **Filter by Form** button on the toolbar or select **Records, Filter, Filter by Form**. A blank form appears, resembling an empty datasheet with a single record line.

2. Click in the field you want to set a criterion for. A down arrow appears for a drop-down list. Click the arrow, and select the value you want from the list. Or, you can type the value directly into the field if you prefer.

3. Enter as many criteria as you like in various fields. Figure 19.3 shows two criteria, including a criterion that uses a less than sign, a mathematical operator (explained in Lesson 20).

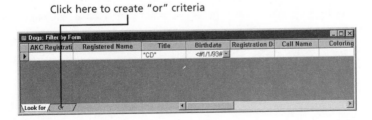

FIGURE 19.3   This query finds all dogs that were born before 1/1/93 and have a CD (Companion Dog) title.

4. If you want to set up an "or" condition, click the **Or** tab at the bottom of the window, and enter the alternative criteria. (Notice that another **Or** tab appears when you fill this one, so you can add multiple "or" conditions.)

5. After you enter your criteria, click the **Apply Filter** button on the toolbar. Your filtered data appears.

As with Filter by Selection, you can remove a filter by clicking the **Remove Filter** button again or by selecting **Records, Remove Filter/Sort**.

SAVING YOUR FILTERED DATA AS A QUERY

Filters are convenient alternatives to creating a simple query from scratch. You can save a filter as a query and use it as you would use a query; it even appears on your Queries list in the Database window. (You'll learn more about working with queries in Lesson 20.)

To save a filter as a query, follow these steps:

1. Display the filter in Filter by Form view.

2. Select **File, Save As Query**, or click the **Save as Query** button on the toolbar. Access asks for the name of the new query.

3. Type a name and click **OK**. Access saves the filter.

CREATING INDEXES

Indexes speed up searches by cataloging the contents of a particular field. The primary key field is automatically indexed. If you frequently search, sort, or filter by using another field, you might want to create an index for that field.

Only Certain Field Types   You can't index a field whose data type is Memo, Hyperlink, or OLE Object.

To index a field, follow these steps:

1. Open the table in Design view.

2. Select the field that you want to index.

3. On the **General** tab, click the **Indexed** field.

4. From the Indexed field's drop-down list appears, select either **Yes (Duplicates OK)** or **Yes (No Duplicates)**, depending on whether that field's content should be unique for each record or not (see Figure 19.4).

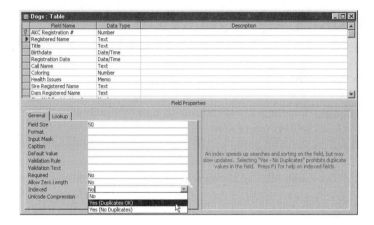

FIGURE 19.4 To index a field, set its Indexed value to one of the Yes choices.

5. Close the Design view of the table.

6. When asked whether you want to save your changes, click **Yes.**

You can't do anything special with an index; an index isn't an object in the same way that tables, databases, and queries are. An index works behind the scenes to speed up your searches but has no independent functions of its own.

In this lesson, you learned how to sort, filter, and index your database. In the next lesson, you will begin learning about queries, a more sophisticated way of isolating and organizing information.

LESSON 20

CREATING A
SIMPLE QUERY

In this lesson, you will create a simple query.

WHAT CAN A QUERY DO?

As you learned in Lesson 19, Access offers many ways to help you narrow down the information you're looking at, including sorting and filtering. A query is simply a more formal way to sort and filter.

Queries enable you to specify

- Which fields you want to see

- In what order the fields should appear

- Filter criteria for each field (see Lesson 19)

- The order in which you want each field sorted (see Lesson 19)

 Saving a Filter When the primary purpose of the query is to filter, you might find it easier to create a filter and save it as a query. See Lesson 19 for details.

The purpose of this lesson is to show you how to create a simple query. In the next lesson, you learn how to modify your query to make it more powerful.

CREATING A QUERY USING THE SIMPLE QUERY WIZARD

The easiest way to create a query is with the Simple Query Wizard, which lets you select the fields you want to display. You don't get to set criteria for including individual records or specify a sort order. (You learn to do those things in Lesson 21.) This kind of simple query is useful when you want to weed out extraneous fields but still want to see every record.

Select Query   The query that the Simple Query Wizard creates is a basic version of a *Select query*, the most common query type. You can select records, sort them, filter them, and perform simple calculations on the results (such as counting and averaging).

Query Wizard   A query wizard asks you questions and then creates a query based on your answers. Access has several query wizards available; you learn about others at the end of this lesson.

To create an easy Select query with the Simple Query Wizard, follow these steps:

1. Open the database you want to work with and click the **Queries** tab.

2. Double-click **Create Query by Using Wizard**. The first dialog box of the Simple Query Wizard appears (see Figure 20.1). This dialog box might look familiar; it's similar to the first screen of the Form Wizard, described in Lesson 14.

3. Choose the table from which you want to select fields from the **Tables/Queries** drop-down list. For example, I'm going to use Dogs.

4. Click a field name in the **Available Fields** list; then click the > button to move it to the **Selected Fields** list. Repeat to move all the fields you want, or move them all at once with the >> button.

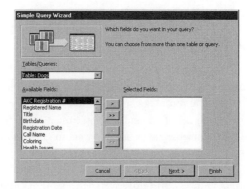

FIGURE 20.1   The Simple Query Wizard first asks what fields you want to include.

5. (Optional) Select another table or query from the **Tables/Queries** list and add some of its fields to the **Selected Fields** list, if you like. When you finish adding fields, click **Next**.

Relationships Required   If you're going to use two or more tables in your query, they must be joined with a relationship. See Lesson 10 to learn how to create relationships between tables.

6. Enter a title for the query in the **What title do you want for your query?** text box. I'm going to call mine Dog Names.

7. Click **Finish** to view the query results. Figure 20.2 shows my results.

But this query is too simple; it has limited usefulness and doesn't show off any of Access's powerful query features. You could get the same results by hiding certain columns in datasheet view! Luckily, there are other means of creating a query that are much more powerful than the query wizard makes it appear, as you'll see in the next lesson. But before you go there, take a look at a few basics that apply to any query.

FIGURE 20.2   Here are the results of my simple query.

SAVING A QUERY

When you create a query, Access saves it automatically. You don't need to do anything special to save it. Just close the query window, and look on the Queries tab of the Database window. You'll see the query on the list.

 Close the Query?   Close a query window the same way you close any window, by clicking its Close button (the × in the top-right corner).

RERUNNING A QUERY

At any time, you can re-run your query. If the data has changed since the last time you ran the query, the changes are represented.

To re-run a query, follow these steps:

1. Open the database containing the query.

2. Click the **Queries** tab in the Database window.

3. Double-click the query you want to re-run, or click it once and then click the **Open** button (see Figure 20.3).

Double-click to open the
Dog Names query.

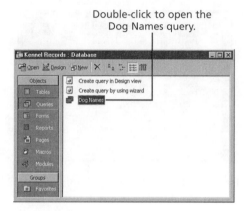

FIGURE 20.3   Redisplay any query by opening it from the
Queries tab.

WORKING WITH QUERY RESULTS

Query results appear in Datasheet view, as shown in Figure 20.2. You can
do anything to the records that you can do in a normal Datasheet view
(see Lesson 12), including copying and deleting records, and changing
field entries.

Say that you wanted to update a sales database to change the Last
Contacted field (a date) to today for every record. From your query results
window, you could make that change. Or perhaps you want to delete all
records for customers who haven't made a purchase in the last two years.
You could delete the records from the query results window, and they
would disappear from the table too.

Of course, with the latter example, it would be easier if the records were
sorted according to the field in question, and the Simple Query Wizard
won't let you sort. However, in Lesson 21, you will learn about some
other, more powerful Query Wizards that let you choose more options.

PRINTING QUERY RESULTS

The query results window not only edits similar to a datasheet but also
prints similar to one. To print the query results, do the following:

   1. Make sure the query results window is active.

2. Select **File**, **Print**, or press **Ctrl+P**. The Print dialog box appears.

3. Select any print options you want (refer to Lesson 11); then click **OK**.

If you don't want to set any print options, you can just click the **Print** button on the toolbar to print, bypassing the Print dialog box.

OTHER QUERY WIZARDS

Access's query features are powerful; they can do amazingly complicated calculations and comparisons on many tables at once. You can create queries with their own dialog boxes for custom entry of special criteria, link a query to external databases (databases in other programs), and much more.

Unfortunately, the process for creating the more powerful queries is quite complicated. It's enough to give casual users a headache. That's why in this book, we stick to the basic Select type of query, which does almost everything average users need to do.

Three other query wizards are available in Access. To run one of them, follow these steps:

1. In the Database window, click **Queries** to display the Queries list.

2. Click the **New** button to open the New Query dialog box (see Figure 20.4).

FIGURE 20.4   You can select another type of query wizard from the New Query dialog box.

3. Click the wizard you want to use.

4. Click **OK**.

5. Follow the Wizard's prompts.

These are the other query types:

- **Crosstab Query Wizard** displays summarized values, such as sums, counts, and averages, from one field. The values are grouped by one set of values listed down the left side of the datasheet as row headings and another set of values listed across the top of the datasheet as column headings.

- **Find Duplicates Query Wizard,** the opposite of Find Unmatched, compares two tables and finds all records that appear in both.

- **Find Unmatched Query Wizard** compares two tables and finds all records that don't appear in both tables (based on comparing certain fields).

In this lesson, you learned to create a simple query and to save, edit, and print query results. In the next lesson, you will see how to modify the query you created.

LESSON 21
DESIGNING YOUR OWN QUERY

In this lesson, you will learn how to open a query in Design view, select fields to include in it, and specify criteria for filtering the records.

WORKING WITH QUERY DESIGN VIEW

In Lesson 20, you created a simple query by using the Simple Query Wizard, which selected and displayed fields from a table. You can do a lot more with your query when you enter Query Design view.

Query Design view is similar to Table Design and Form Design views, both of which you've encountered earlier in this book. In Query Design view, you can change the rules that govern your query results.

OPENING A QUERY IN QUERY DESIGN VIEW

To open an existing query in Query Design view, follow these steps:

1. Open the database that contains the query you want to edit.

2. Click the **Queries** object in the Object Bar.

3. Click the query you want to edit; then click the **Design** button.

Figure 21.1 shows the query created in Lesson 20 in Query Design view. You'll learn how to edit it in this lesson.

This query uses only one table.

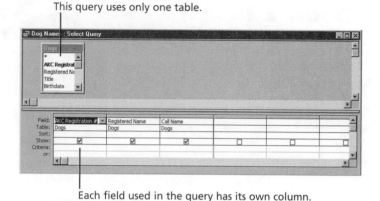

Each field used in the query has its own column.

FIGURE 21.1   In Query Design view, you can edit a query you've created.

STARTING A NEW QUERY IN QUERY DESIGN VIEW

Rather than use the Simple Query Wizard to begin your query, as you did in Lesson 20, you can begin a query from scratch in Query Design view. As you become more familiar with Access queries, you might find this method faster and easier than using a wizard.

To begin a new query in Query Design view, follow these steps:

1. Open the database in which you want the query.

2. Click the **Queries** object in the Database window.

3. Double-click **Create query in Design View**. The Show Table dialog box appears, listing all the tables in the database (see Figure 21.2).

4. Click a table you want to work with; then click the **Add** button. Repeat for each table you want to add. It's best to create a relationship between the tables in advance, using the Relationships window (see Lesson 10).

5. Click **Close** when you finish adding tables. The Query Design view window opens, as in Figure 21.1, except there won't be any fields selected yet.

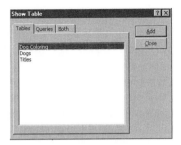

FIGURE 21.2 Choose which tables you want to include in the query.

ADDING FIELDS TO A QUERY

If you created your query from scratch (as in the preceding steps), the first thing you need to do is add the fields you want to work with. You can also use this same procedure to add fields to an existing query.

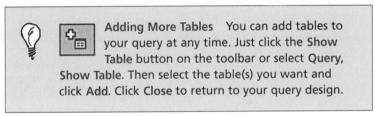

Adding More Tables You can add tables to your query at any time. Just click the **Show Table** button on the toolbar or select **Query, Show Table**. Then select the table(s) you want and click **Add**. Click **Close** to return to your query design.

You can add a field to a query in three ways. All methods are easy; try all of them to see which you prefer. Here's the first method:

1. Click in the Table row of the first blank column. A down-arrow button appears, indicating that a drop-down list is available.

2. Open the drop-down list and select a table. The tables available on the list are the same as the table windows that appear at the top of the query design window.

Only One Table?   If you are using only one table in the query, you can skip the first two steps in this procedure.

3. Click in the Field row directly above the table name you just selected. A down-arrow button appears, indicating that a drop-down list is available.

4. Open the drop-down list and select a field. The fields listed come from the tables you selected for the query. The field's name appears in the Field row, in the column where you selected it.

Here's the second method of adding a field:

1. Scroll through the list of fields in the desired table window at the top of the Query Design box, until you find the field you want to add.

2. Click the field name and drag it into the Field row of the first empty column. The field's name appears where you dragged it.

The third method is to simply double-click the field name in the field list. It moves to the first available slot in the query grid.

DELETING A FIELD

There are two ways to delete a field from your query:

• Click anywhere in the column and select **Edit, Delete Columns**.

• Position the mouse pointer directly above the column so that the pointer turns into a down-pointing black arrow. Then, click to select the entire column and press **Delete**, or click the **Cut** button on the toolbar.

Cut versus Delete   If you cut the column rather than delete it, you can paste it back into the query. Just select the column where you want it, and then click the Paste button or choose Edit, Paste. Be careful, though; the pasted column replaces the selected one—the selected column doesn't move over to make room for it. Select an empty column if you don't want to replace an existing one.

ADDING CRITERIA

Criteria is familiar to you if you read Lesson 19, which deals with filters. Criteria enable you to choose which records appear in your query results. For example, I could limit my list of dogs to those whose birth dates were before 1/1/94.

 Filters versus Queries   If the primary reason for creating the query is to filter, you might want to create the filter part first by using one of the procedures described in Lesson 19, and then save the filter as a query. You can open that query in Query Design view and fine-tune it as needed.

To set criteria for a field that you've added to your query, follow these steps:

1. In Query Design view, click the Criteria row in the desired field's column.

2. Type the criteria you want to use (see Figure 21.3). Table 21.1 provides some examples you could have entered in Figure 21.3 and the subsequent results.

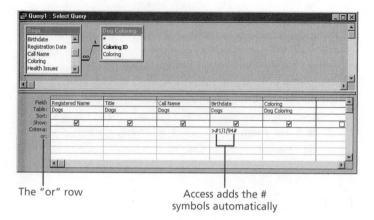

The "or" row   Access adds the #
                                symbols automatically

FIGURE 21.3   Enter criteria into the Criteria row in the appropriate field's column.

In Figure 21.3, Access added # symbols because I was entering a date. For other types of criteria, Access adds other symbols, such as quotation marks around a text or number string.

TABLE 21.1   SAMPLE CRITERIA FOR QUERIES

ENTER THIS	TO GET RECORDS THAT MATCH THIS
1/1/93	Exactly 1/1/93
<1/1/93	Before 1/1/93
>1/1/93	After 1/1/93
>=1/1/93	1/1/93 or after
<=1/1/93	1/1/93 or before
Not <1/1/93	Not before 1/1/93
Not >1/1/93	Not after 1/1/93

Text, Too   You can also enter text as a criteria. The < and > (before and after) operators apply to alphabetical order with text. For instance, <C finds text that begins with A or B.

Did you notice the "or" row below the Criteria row in Figure 21.3? You can enter more criteria by using that line. The query finds records where any of the criteria is true. When you enter criteria into the "or" row, another "or" row appears, so you can enter more.

What About And? When you have two criteria that must both be true, you can put them together in a single Criteria row, joining them with the word And. For instance, you might want birth dates between 12/1/93 and 12/1/95. All the dates would appear in a single Criteria row, like this: >12/1/93 And <12/1/95.

VIEWING QUERY RESULTS

When you're ready to see the results of your query, click the **Run** button or choose **Query**, **Run**. Your results appear in a window that resembles a datasheet (see Figure 21.4).

Only records where the Birthdate
was after 1/1/94 appear.

Registered Name	Title	Call Name	Birthdate	Coloring
Rapporlee Gold Star	CD	Ashley	5/19/94	Blue
Nightingale Rhapsody	OTCH	Earl	5/1/95	Bi-black
Russian Blue	CH	Baby	7/2/98	Tricolor
King of the Hill	CD	Champ	2/3/94	Blue
Happiglade Tornado	UD	Ruby	2/3/94	Sable
Carrolton Make a Wish	CD	Boopsie	9/12/95	Sable
Brazen Puppy Gold	None	Loudmouth	3/3/96	Blue

Record: 1 of 7

FIGURE 21.4 The results of a kennel query based on birth dates.

In this lesson, you learned how to choose the fields for a query and specify criteria. In the next lesson, you will learn how to sort the records in a query, hide certain fields, and include calculated fields.

LESSON 22

CUSTOMIZING A QUERY

In this lesson, you will learn how to sort the results of a query, include hidden fields in a query, and add a calculated field.

SORTING A FIELD IN A QUERY

You've already seen that you can sort the records in a table with the **Records, Sort** command or the **Sort** buttons on the toolbar. Your query results appear in table format, and you can sort your results the same way. But you can also specify a particular sorting in Query Design view so that the sorting takes place automatically when the query runs. To do so from Query Design view, follow these steps:

1. Click in the sort row for the field you want to sort. A down arrow for a drop–down list appears.

2. Open the drop–down list and select **Ascending** or **Descending** (see Figure 22.1).

Later, if you want to cancel sorting for this field, repeat these steps but select **(not sorted)**. Refer to Lesson 19 for more information about sorting.

Choose a sort order.

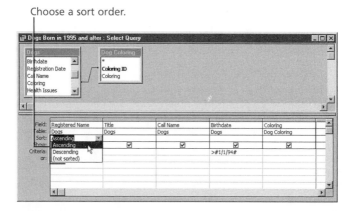

FIGURE 22.1   Choose Ascending or Descending to sort records by that field.

 Sorting by Multiple Fields   If you choose a sort order for more than one field in the query, Access sorts from left to right, starting with the leftmost field in the Query Design window.

 Sorting by a Hidden Field   If you want the records sorted according to a field that's not part of the query, include that field in the query and then remove the checkmark from its Show line to hide it, as explained in the following section.

SHOWING OR HIDING A FIELD

Some fields are included only so that you can filter or sort based on them. You might not necessarily be interested in seeing those fields in the query results, however. For instance, you might want to limit your query to all dogs born before 8/5/93, but you don't want each dog's birth date to appear in the query.

To exclude a field from appearing in the query results, deselect the check box in the Show row (see Figure 22.2). To include it again, select the check box again.

Show check box

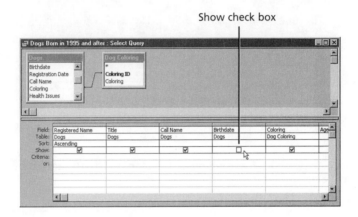

FIGURE 22.2   You can control which fields appear in the query results with the Show check box in each column.

ADDING A CALCULATED FIELD

Calculated fields are helpful when you need to compute a value in your database by performing a math function on one or more fields' contents. For example, you might want to calculate a 5 percent sales tax based on the price of each item you sell. Or, in our kennel example, you might want to calculate each dog's current age by subtracting its birth date from the current date.

To add a calculated field, such as a field that calculates sales tax, follow these steps:

1. Open the query in Design view if it's not already open there.

2. In an empty column, type an expression in the Field row. If the expression includes a field name, put brackets around it. For example, to multiply the Price field by .05, type **[Price]*.05**.

Expression Builder   To use functions (similar to those in Excel) in your calculation, click the **Build** button on the toolbar to open the Expression Builder window. Then choose the functions, constants, operators, and other items from the Expression Builder. See the Access Help system for details.

3. Press **Enter** or move to another cell. Access adds a name for the expression, such as `Expr1`. For example, the expression might now read `Expr1:[Price]*.05`.

4. Click in the cell again and highlight the expression name (for example, `Expr1`).

5. Type a more descriptive name, such as **Tax**.

Look at another example—calculating each dog's age in the kennel database. This is a more complicated expression because it involves using a built-in function: `Now()-[Birthdate]/365`. This formula subtracts the Birthdate field's value from today's date, and then divides the result (in days) by 365 to give you the number of years.

To set this up by using the Expression Builder, follow these steps:

1. Click in an empty column's Field cell.

2. Click the **Build** button on the toolbar to open the Expression Builder.

3. In the left–hand list, double–click **Functions** to display the functions. Then click **Built–In Functions**. The function categories appear in the middle list.

4. In the middle list, click **Date/Time**.

5. In the right pane, click **Now**.

6. Click the **Paste** button, pasting the function in the Expression list at the top of the window (see Figure 22.3).

Pasted items appear in   Click Paste to select
the Expression list   the chosen function

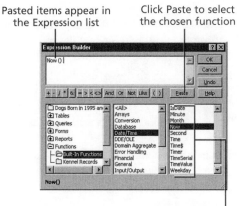

Choose a function

FIGURE 22.3   Start your expression by pasting the Now() function
into it.

7. Type a dash or click the minus sign (–) button.

8. In the leftmost list, double–click the **Tables** folder, and then click
the name of the table containing the field (for example, Dogs).

9. In the middle list, select the field you want to use.

10. Click **Paste** to add the field to the expression.

11. Type a / or click the / button. (This means "divided by.")

12. Type 365.

13. In the expression, type parentheses around the part that subtracts
the birth date from the current date. Your formula should now
resemble this:

```
(Now()[Dogs]![Birthdate])/365
```

Order of Precedence Alert   By default, multiplication
and division are calculated first in expressions, and
then addition and subtraction. However, in this formula you want the subtraction to be done first. That's
why step 13 is necessary.

14. Click **OK** to close the Expression Builder.

15. Click in the expression to move the insertion point there, and then edit it to change Expr1 to **Age**. This renames the field to a more meaningful name.

16. Right–click the expression and choose **Properties**.

17. On the **General** page, open the **Format** drop–down list and choose **Fixed**.

18. Type **0** in the Decimal Places field (see Figure 22.4).

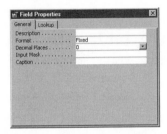

FIGURE **22.4**   Set the new field for a fixed number of decimal places, and set that fixed number to zero.

19. Close the property sheet.

20. Run the query to test your work.

In this lesson, you learned how to sort records from a query, and how to exclude some fields from appearing in the query results. You also learned to place calculated fields in queries. In the next lesson, you will learn how to create a simple, attractive report suitable for printing and distribution to others.

LESSON 23
CREATING A
SIMPLE REPORT

In this lesson, you will learn how to create reports in Access by using the AutoReport and Report wizards.

WHY CREATE REPORTS?

You've seen many ways to organize and view your data, but until now each method has focused on onscreen use. Forms help with data entry onscreen, and queries help you find information and display the results onscreen.

You can print any table, form, or query, but the results will be less than professional looking because those tools aren't designed to be printed. Reports, on the other hand, are designed specifically to be printed and shared with other people. With a report, you can generate professional results that you can be proud of, whether you're distributing them on paper or publishing them on the Internet.

You can create a report in several ways, ranging from easy-but-limited (AutoReport) to difficult-but-very-flexible (Report Design view). The intermediate choice is the Report Wizard, which offers some flexibility along with a fairly easy procedure.

USING AUTOREPORT TO CREATE A REPORT

If you want a plain, no-frills report based on a single table or query, AutoReport is for you. You can go back and improve its appearance later, when you learn about customizing reports in Lesson 24.

You can create a tabular or columnar report. A tabular report resembles a datasheet, and a columnar report resembles a form. They are equally easy to create.

To create a report with AutoReport, follow these steps:

1. Open the database containing the table or query on which you want to report.

2. Click the **Reports** object in the Database window, and click the **New** button. The New Report dialog box appears (see Figure 23.1).

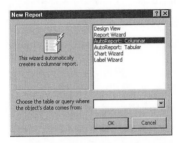

FIGURE 23.1   Choose one of the AutoReports from this window.

3. Select **AutoReport: Columnar** or **AutoReport: Tabular**.

4. In the drop-down list at the bottom of the dialog box, select the table or query on which you want to base the report.

Multiple Tables?   AutoReports can use only one table or query. If you want to create an AutoReport that uses several tables, first create a query based on those tables, and then base the AutoReport on the query.

5. Click **OK**. The report appears in Print Preview. See the "Viewing and Printing Reports in Print Preview" section later in this lesson to learn what to do next.

AutoReport's output isn't much better than a raw printout from a table or form, as you can see in Print Preview. If you want a better-looking report, try the Report Wizard.

CREATING A REPORT WITH THE REPORT WIZARD

The Report Wizard offers a good compromise between ease-of-use and flexibility. With the Report Wizard, you can use multiple tables and queries and choose a layout and format for your report. Follow these steps to create a report with Report Wizard:

1. Open the database containing the table or query on which you want to report.

2. Click the **Reports** tab in the Database window.

3. Double-click **Create report by using wizard** to start the Report Wizard (see Figure 23.2).

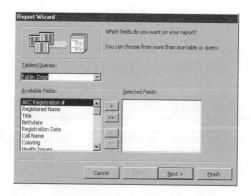

FIGURE 23.2   The first Report Wizard dialog box.

4. From the **Tables/Queries** drop-down list, select a table or query from which you want to include fields.

5. Click a field in the **Available Fields** list, and then click the > button to move it to the **Selected Fields** list. Repeat this step to select all the fields you want, or click >> to move all the fields over at once.

6. If desired, select another table or query from the **Tables/Queries** list and repeat step 5. The tables you choose should have relationships between them, so your data will match up on the report. When you finish selecting fields, click **Next**. The wizard's next dialog box appears (see Figure 23.3).

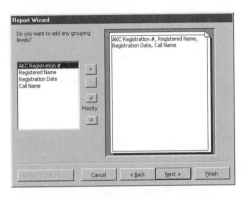

FIGURE 23.3   Set your report's grouping.

7. If you want the records grouped by any of the fields you selected, click the field, and then click the > button. You can select several grouping levels in the order you want them. Then click **Next** to move on.

 Grouping?   By default, there are no groups. You have to select a field and click the > button to create a group. Grouping sets off each group on the report. If you use a field to group, the **Grouping Options** button becomes active, and you can click it to specify precise grouping settings.

8. You're asked what sort order you want to use (see Figure 23.4). If you want sorted records, open the top drop-down list and select a field to sort by. Select up to four sorts from the drop-down lists; then click **Next**.

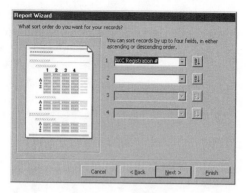

FIGURE 23.4   Set the sort order.

    Ascending or Descending?   By default, the sort is in ascending order (A–Z). Click the **AZ** button next to the box to change the sort order to descending (Z–A) if you like.

9. In the next dialog box (see Figure 23.5), choose a layout option from the **Layout** section. When you click an option button, the sample in the box changes to show your selection.

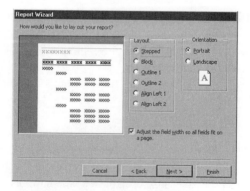

FIGURE 23.5   Choose the layout of your report.

Where Are All the Layouts? If you don't choose any groupings in your report, your layout choices are limited to three: **Columnar, Tabular,** and **Justified.** The layouts shown in Figure 23.5 are unique to grouped reports.

10. Choose which orientation your printed report will have: **Portrait** (across the narrow edge of the paper) or **Landscape** (across the wide edge of the paper). Then click **Next** to continue.

11. In the next wizard dialog box, you're asked to choose a report style. Several are listed; click one to see a sample of it, and then click **Next** when you're satisfied with your choice.

12. You're asked for a report title. Enter one in the **Report** text box, and click **Finish** to see your report in Print Preview (see Figure 23.6).

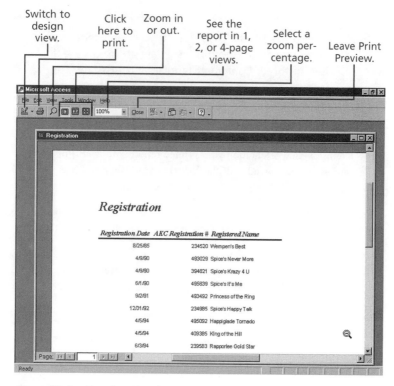

FIGURE 23.6   Here's a simple report with no grouping.

VIEWING AND PRINTING REPORTS IN PRINT PREVIEW

When you create a report with either the Report Wizard or AutoReport, the report appears in Print Preview (as shown in Figure 23.6). From here, you can print the report, if you're happy with it, or go to Report Design view to make changes. (You'll learn more about this in Lesson 24.)

 If you want to print the report and specify any print options (such as number of copies), choose **File, Print**. If you want a quick hard copy, click the toolbar's **Print** button. To go to Report Design view, choose **View, Design View**.

In this lesson, you learned how to create and print a simple report. In the next lesson, you will learn how to work in Report Design view to customize your report.

LESSON 24

CUSTOMIZING A REPORT

In this lesson, you will learn how to use Report Design view to make your reports more attractive.

ENTERING REPORT DESIGN VIEW

When you finish previewing a report you've created, just close Print Preview to close the report, or switch to Design View from the **View** menu. If you want to come back to Report Design view later, perform these steps from the Database window:

1. Click the **Reports** object in the database window.

2. Click the report you want to modify.

3. Click the **Design** button. The report appears in Design view, as shown in Figure 24.1.

As you can see in Figure 24.1, the Report Header section shows the report title, whereas the Page Header shows the column labels for the report. The Detail area lists the fields that you chose to print under those columns. And the Page Footer contains a formula that prints the current date and time.

Report Design view might seem familiar to you; it looks similar to Form Design view. Almost everything you learned about editing forms in Lessons 15 and 17 applies also to reports. Just as in Form Design view, Report Design contains a toolbox of common editing tools, where you can add all the special elements that you learned about in Lesson 16.

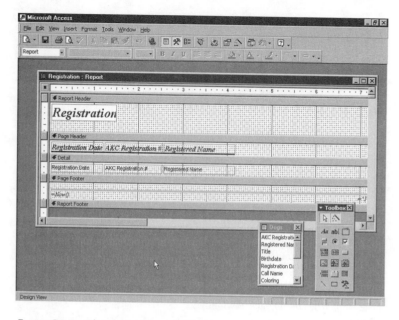

FIGURE 24.1 The report created in the previous lesson, in Report Design view.

 Command Button on a Report? Access lets you place any type of control on a report, even those that are frankly silly, like command buttons or combo boxes. It's best, however, to stick to text boxes, labels, and graphics on reports.

WORKING WITH CONTROLS ON YOUR REPORT

Working with report controls in Report Design view is exactly the same as working with controls in Form Design view. Turn back to Lesson 15 for the full story, or follow the brief review here:

- **Selecting controls.** Just as in Form Design view, you select a control on your report by clicking it. Selection handles (little squares in the corners) appear around it. See Lesson 15 for more details.

- **Moving objects.** To move a control, first select it. Next, position the mouse pointer over a border so the pointer turns into an open black hand. Then, click and drag the control to a new location.

Moving Controls Between Sections You can't drag an object to a different section, but you can cut and paste it. Select the object and press **Ctrl+X** to cut it. Then, click the title of the section where you want to move it, and press **Ctrl+V** to paste it in the newly selected section.

- **Resizing controls.** First, select the control. Then, position the mouse pointer over a selection handle and drag it to resize the object.

- **Formatting text box controls.** Use the **Font** and **Font Size** drop-down lists on the toolbar to choose fonts; then use the **Bold, Italic,** and **Underline** toolbar buttons to set special attributes.

You can also add graphic lines and images to reports, just as you do with forms. Refer back to Lesson 17, "Adding Graphics to Forms."

Access on the Web You can assign hyperlinks to objects on your forms and reports, as you'll learn in Lesson 27. Hyperlinks aren't of much use on the printouts, of course, but if you save a report in Microsoft Word format, the hyperlinks can be activated when you open the document in Word.

Adding and Removing Controls

You can add more controls to your report at any time. Follow these steps:

1. If you don't see the field list, choose **View, Field List,** or click the **Field List** button on the toolbar. A floating box appears, listing all the fields in the table or query you're using.

2. Drag any field from the field list into the report, where it becomes a control, by default a text box. Place it anywhere in the Detail area that you want.

Don't worry if the control isn't in the right place or overlaps another control; you'll learn how to fix that in the next section. To delete a control, select it by clicking it, and then press **Delete**. Deleting a control from the report doesn't delete the field from the table.

ARRANGING YOUR NEW CONTROLS

When you add a control to your report, you're actually adding two things—a label and a text box. These two elements are bound together: the label describes the text box, and the text box represents the actual field that will be used (see Figure 24.2). You can change the text in the label without affecting the text box; for instance, you could change the label on the Coloring field to Dog Color without affecting the contents. To change a label, just click it and retype.

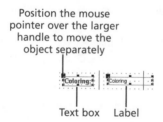

Position the mouse
pointer over the larger
handle to move the
object separately

Text box   Label

FIGURE 24.2   The text box and its label.

🖑 By default, when you move the text box, the label follows. When you position the mouse over the border of the text box and the pointer changes to an open hand, it's your signal that the label will follow the text box when you drag it.

🖑 However, you can also move the text box and the label separately. Notice that in the upper-left corner of each control is a selection handle (square) that's bigger than the others. When you position the mouse pointer over that handle, the cursor becomes a pointing hand. It's your signal that you can click and drag the object separately from the other.

Moving the label separately can come in handy when you don't want the label to appear in its default position (to the left of the text box). For instance, you might want the label to appear above the text box.

ADDING LABELS

In the preceding section, you saw how to add a pair of controls—a text box and an attached label. But you can also add labels by themselves, with extra text in them that's not necessarily associated with a particular field—for instance, an informational note about the report in general. Just click the **Label** button in the Toolbox. Then, click anywhere on the report and start typing. When you finish, click anywhere outside the label.

ADDING A CALCULATED TEXT BOX

Text boxes most commonly display data from fields, as you've seen in this lesson. However, text boxes have another purpose—they can also hold calculations based on values in different fields.

Creating a calculated text box is a bit complicated: First, you have to create an unbound text box (that is, one that's not associated with any particular field), and then you have to enter the calculation into the text box. Follow these steps:

1. Click the **Text Box** tool in the Toolbox, and click and drag on the report to create a text box.

2. Change the label to reflect what's going in the text box. For instance, if it's **Sales Tax**, change the label accordingly. Position the label where you want it.

3. Click in the text box and type the formula you want calculated. (See the following section for guidance.)

4. Click anywhere outside the text box when you finish.

The formulas you enter into your calculated text box use standard mathematical controls:

+	Add
−	Subtract
*	Multiply
/	Divide

All formulas begin with an equal sign (=), and all field names are in square brackets ([ ]). Here are some examples:

- To calculate a total price by multiplying the value in the Quantity field by the value in the Price field, enter **=[Quantity]*[Price]**.

- To calculate a 25 percent discount off the value in the Cost field, enter **=[Cost]*.075**.

- To add the total of the values in three fields, enter **[Field1]+[Field2]+[Field3]**.

More Room   If you run out of room in the text box when typing your formula, press **Shift+F2** to open a Zoom box, where there's more room.

In this lesson, you learned how to customize your report by adding and removing objects, moving them around, and creating calculations. In the next lesson, you will see how to create a chart based on a table or query in your database.

LESSON 25

WORKING WITH RELATED TABLES

In this chapter, you will learn how to use related tables in forms, queries, and reports.

WHAT GOOD ARE RELATED TABLES?

When you created your database in the beginning of this book, I advised you to create relationships between tables. (You created the relationships in Lesson 10.) You might have wondered why you were doing this—what good it would do you. In this lesson, I'll show you some of the ways related tables help you manage your data.

A relationship links two tables by connecting matching fields. This makes it possible to break out repetitive or peripheral information into its own table, while still using that information in the main table.

For example, in Figure 25.1, the Titles and the Dog Coloring tables support the main table (Dogs) by providing lists of valid values for certain fields. The Titles table contains a list of all the titles a dog might have, and the Dog Coloring table contains a list of all the AKC-registerable colorings that a dog of the particular breed might have.

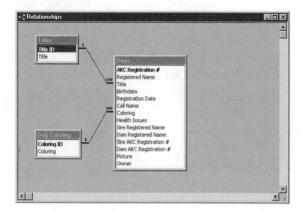

FIGURE 25.1   Open the Relationships window (Tools, Relationships) to view the current relationships.

In more sophisticated databases, you might have many relationships among tables. See if you can trace and understand all the relationships in Figure 25.2, a Sales database.

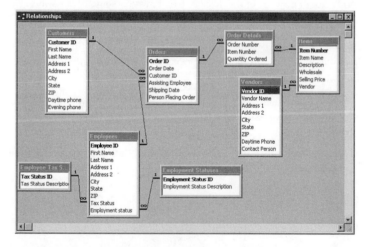

FIGURE 25.2   Businesses with customers, vendors, inventory, and employees can have a complex system of relationships.

VIEWING RELATED DATA IN DATASHEET VIEW

When looking at a table in Datasheet view, you can quickly view information from a related table. (This is one of the many great new features in Access 2000.) Suppose that you are looking at the Titles table (from Figure 25.1) in Datasheet view. Plus signs appear next to each record. When you click a plus sign, a mini-table appears, listing all the records from the related table with the same value (see Figure 25.3).

These records from Dogs contain
a value of 0 in the Title field.

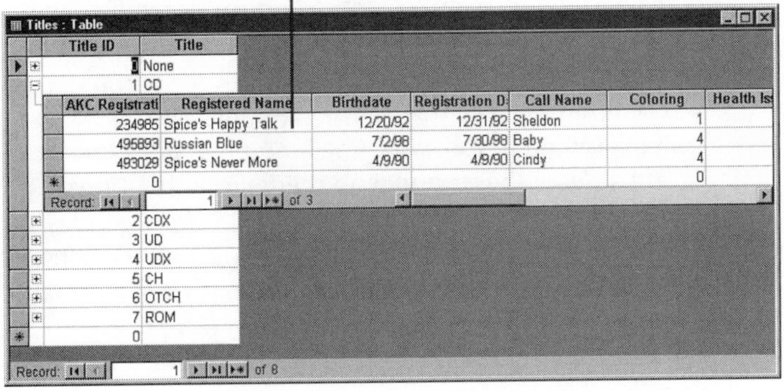

FIGURE 25.3   Display related records in the linked table by clicking a plus sign next to a record.

When related records are displayed, the plus sign turns into a minus sign. Click that minus sign to rehide the related records.

CREATING MULTITABLE QUERIES

Multitable queries are used for pulling information from more than one table at the same time. You can then use that information in reports, forms, or other queries, or you can simply view the information in a table-like query results window.

To create a multitable query, create a new query through Design view (refer to Lesson 21). In the Show Table dialog box, add more than one table before you click **Close**. You'll then have multiple tables to pull fields from. If the tables aren't already linked, create a temporary link between them by dragging a field from one table to its matching field in the other table, just as you did in the Relationships window in Lesson 10. Then proceed normally to finish the query, as you learned in Lesson 21.

A Use for a Multitable Query When you join two tables, such as Titles and Dogs from Figure 25.1, you usually join them by number fields. In Figure 25.1, Title ID in the Titles table is joined to Title in the Dogs table. That means that a number, not a descriptive name, appears in the Dogs table for each dog's title. I don't have all the title ID numbers memorized, so it's hard for me to tell what title a dog has. But I can create a query that includes all the fields in the Dogs table except Title, plus the Title field from the Titles table (which contains descriptive text). Then I can use that query's results instead of the Dogs table to create forms and reports.

CREATING MULTITABLE FORMS

You learned in the preceding section how you can create a query that includes fields from more than one table—that's the easiest way to create a multitable form. Just create the query, and then base the form on the query.

Subform A subform isn't another type of database object—it's just a form placed as an object on another form. You can make a form into a subform by dragging it to another form that's open in Design view.

Another way is to create a form with an embedded subform. The subform can contain data from any related table. For example, on a Customers form, you could include a subform listing all the orders that customer has placed.

To create a form with an embedded subform, follow these steps:

1. Start a new form by using the Form Wizard. To do so, from the Database window, click the **Forms** tab, and then double-click **Create form by using wizard**.

2. In the Form Wizard's first dialog box, choose a table or query, and then select the fields you want to use from it. (You learned this in Lesson 14.)

3. Rather than move on, choose the second table or query from the **Tables/Queries** drop-down list, and select fields from it too (see Figure 25.4).

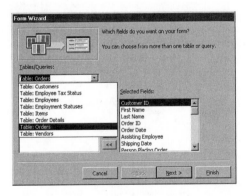

FIGURE 25.4   After selecting fields for one table, choose another one and select more fields before clicking **Next**.

  Tables must be linked   If you select two tables that aren't already linked, the Form Wizard will give you a warning message at this point, and you will have to exit the Wizard and set up a link between the tables you want to use.

4. Continue changing tables/queries and selecting more fields until you have all the fields you need. Then click **Next**.

5. The wizard asks how you want to view your data. Choose one table from the list to be the main form's data source; the other one will be the subform's data source (see Figure 25.5).

 Linked Forms These steps show you how to create a form with a subform, but you might prefer to have two separate forms to hold the data from the two tables or queries. If you prefer this, click the **Linked** Forms button in the wizard dialog box in Figure 25.5. Then complete with the wizard normally, as you learned in Lesson 14.

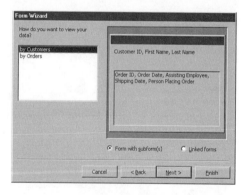

FIGURE 25.5   Choose how you want the data from the tables to be displayed.

6. Click **Next**.

7. The wizard then asks about the format for the subform. Choose **Tabular** (similar to a table in Word) or **Datasheet** (similar to a spreadsheet in Excel) and click **Next**.

8. Choose a form style, and click **Next**.

9. Enter titles for your form and your subform. (They will be saved as separate forms in your database.) Then click **Finish**. Your form appears, as in Figure 25.6.

Main form   Subform

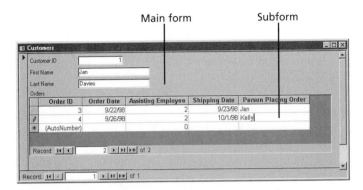

FIGURE 25.6 This form contains fields from one table in the main form and another table in the subform.

CREATING MULTITABLE REPORTS

Just as with forms, you can create reports that use multiple tables or queries. The process for doing so is almost exactly the same as that for creating a single-table report, which you learned in Lesson 23. Here's a quick review:

1. Create the relationships between the tables. See Lesson 10.

2. Start a new report by using the Report Wizard. (In the Database window, click the **Reports** tab, and then double-click **Create report by using wizard**.)

3. Select the fields from the first table you want to use.

4. From the **Tables/Queries** drop-down list, select a different table or query. Then select fields from it. This is similar to what you did with forms back in Figure 25.4.

5. When you are finished, click **Next**.

6. When asked how you want to view your data, choose one of the tables. This is the same as the selection you made for forms back in Figure 25.5. Then click **Next**.

7. Continue with the wizard as usual, adding grouping, sorting, and so on. Refer to Lesson 23 if needed.

8. When you reach the end of the wizard's process, click **Finish** to create your report.

In this lesson, you learned how to create queries, forms, and reports based on more than one related table. In the next lesson, you will learn how to create a chart from your data.

LESSON 26

CREATING A CHART

In this lesson, you will learn how to create a chart based on data in your database.

THE CHART ADVANTAGE

Have you ever noticed how people's eyes glaze over when you present them with a stack of statistics? Your message will come across more clearly if you present your information in a format that's easy to understand, such as a chart. One glance at a chart can communicate the message contained in a hundred pages of raw data.

Say that I want to know which colors of dogs my kennel owns the most of. I could print a report that lists all the dogs and their colorings, manually count how many of each color there are, and divide each color total by the total number of dogs. This technique would give me the percentage of each color. Creating a chart that shows the percentage of each coloring would be much easier.

Charts are also good for tracking information over time. For instance, in a sales organization, you could chart the sales volume for each sales person by month, or you could chart how many units of each product you sell per month (or week, or year).

CREATING A CHART

A chart control can be inserted on a report or a form; in this lesson you will learn how to create a chart report, which is simply a report with a single chart control on it. Just follow along with the wizard.

The Chart Wizard works basically the same for all charts, but the dialog boxes vary a little. So first, let's create a simple pie chart based on a query, and then try a bar chart.

CREATING A SIMPLE PIE CHART

A pie chart is good for relating parts to a whole. To create a pie chart, follow these steps:

1. Open the database that contains the table or query that you want to chart.

2. Click the **Reports** tab in the database window, and then click the **New** button. The New Report dialog box appears.

3. Select **Chart Wizard**.

4. Open the drop-down list at the bottom of the dialog box and select the table or query that contains the data you want to chart (the Employee Sales by Country query from Northwind is a good choice). Then click **OK**, and the Chart Wizard starts (see Figure 26.1).

Click here to move a selected field to the Fields for Chart list.

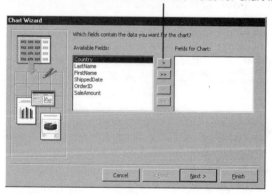

FIGURE 26.1   The Chart Wizard first asks which fields you want to include.

 Don't Select Too Many!   Select exactly two fields for a pie chart (one for labels and one for data) or two or more fields for most other chart types. Otherwise, either all the fields won't show up on the chart, or the chart will look crowded.

5. Select a field from the **Available Fields** list, and click the > button to move it to the **Fields for Chart** list. Because I'm making a pie chart, which can accommodate only two fields (the data and the label), I'll just select **Coloring Country** and **Sale Amount**. Click **Next** to move on.

6. Choose which chart type you want (see Figure 26.2). Click one of the pie chart pictures and read the description that appears. Notice that most chart types have both three-dimensional and two-dimensional versions. When you're satisfied with your choice, click **Next**.

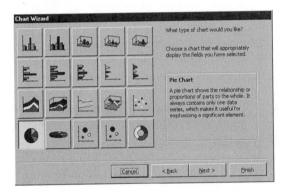

FIGURE **26.2**   Select the chart type.

7. Next you'll see a layout dialog box. This dialog box is important with more complicated charts, but with a pie chart, there's nothing much to do, so just click **Next** to move on.

8. The last Chart Wizard dialog box asks for a title. Enter one.

9. Click **Yes, Display A Legend** or **No, Don't Display A Legend**. (I recommend **Yes** if you don't know which to pick.) Then click **Finish**. Your chart appears in Print Preview; mine is shown in Figure 26.3.

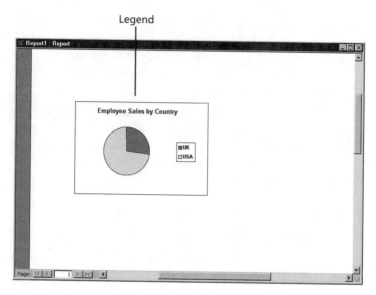

FIGURE 26.3   The finished pie chart.

Line and bar charts both show data over time. For instance, you might show your sales over several years. Let's do that in the following steps:

1. Follow the first three steps of the procedure in "Creating a Simple Pie Chart" earlier in this lesson, so that the New Report dialog box is displayed and you've chosen Chart Wizard as the report type.

2. Choose the table or query you want to work with from the drop-down list. For the Northwind Traders database example, I'm picking **Employee Sales By Country**. Then click **OK**, and the first dialog box of the Chart Wizard appears.

3. Add the fields you want to work with to the **Fields for Chart** list, as you did with the pie chart. You'll want to pick at least two fields because a bar chart has two axes (for instance, I'm picking Country and Sale Amount). Then click **Next**.

4. You'll be asked to select a chart type (as in Figure 26.2). Click one of the bar charts and then click **Next**. You'll see the layout dialog box.

5. If the fields aren't correct, drag them from the chart back to the right side of the dialog box to remove them from the chart, and then drag the correct fields onto the correct spots. When everything is correct, click Next.

6. In the next box that appears, enter a title, choose whether to use a legend (not necessary for the example data), and then click Finish.

7. Depending on the table or query you used, you might be asked to enter extra information. For example, I was asked to input a start date and an end date. I used 1/1/97 as the beginning and 1/1/99 as the ending date.

After you answer all the questions, your chart appears. Mine is shown in Figure 26.4.

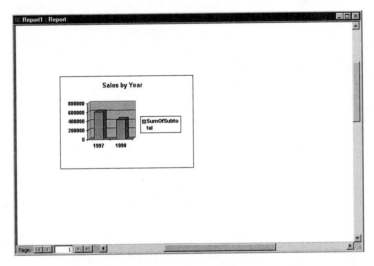

FIGURE 26.4   A simple bar chart created with the Northwind Traders database that comes with Access.

USING PRINT PREVIEW

The procedure for working with a chart report in Print Preview is exactly the same as the procedure you learned in Lesson 23. You can print by clicking the **Print** button or close Print Preview by clicking the **Close** button.

SAVING A CHART REPORT

To save a chart report, just exit from Print Preview by clicking the **Close** button. You'll get a message asking if you want to save the changes to your report. Click **Yes**, and you'll be prompted for a name. Type the chart's name as you want it to appear on the Reports tab of the Database window, and then click **OK**. Access puts you into Design view, where you can modify your chart.

In this lesson, you learned to create, print, and save a chart report. In the next lesson, you will learn how to use Access with the Internet.

Lesson 27

Using Access on the Internet

In this lesson, you will learn how to take advantage of Access 2000's new Internet capabilities to link your work to the Internet.

Some Internet Basics

The Internet is a vast collection of connected computer networks, and the most popular component of it is the World Wide Web. Most Web files are stored in a format known as *Hypertext Markup Language*, or HTML.

Access provides two ways to interact with Internet: incoming and outgoing. In other words, you can provide Access information to people who use the Internet, or you can provide Internet information to people who use your Access database.

To provide information to incoming users (that is, visitors to your Web site), you can make parts of your database available by saving tables in HTML format and copying the files to an Internet host (a computer that's directly connected to the Internet). If your company provides an Internet connection through its local area network (LAN), it probably also has a host computer where you can save HTML files somewhere on the network. If you use a modem to connect to the Internet, the local host that you dial into might provide space on its server for your HTML files.

You can also set up hyperlinks to other URLs within a database, so that your database users can have outgoing access to Web sites. When users click a hyperlink as they use the database, their Web browser programs open in a separate window and the specified URL is displayed.

Uniform Resource Locator (URL)   An URL is a Web address. It's similar to a phone number for the Internet. Most URLs begin with http://, followed by the site's name—for instance, http://www.mcp.com. Some URLs also contain specific directory and file-names, similar to this: http://www.mcp.com/Pub/index.htm. Pub/ is a directory, and index.htm is a file name.

Hyperlink   A hyperlink is a bit of text or a picture that you can click to access a specific URL quickly. When you click on a hyperlink, your Web browser program opens (if you have one set up) and the specified URL's data is displayed.

SAVING AS A WEB PAGE

You can save various Access database objects in HTML format, but you will probably find it most useful to save your tables. The tables contain your data, and it's your data that Web visitors will be most interested in seeing.

Access 2000 treats HTML similar to any other data format, so it's easy to save your work as an HTML file. Follow these steps:

1. In the Database window, select the object you want to export.

2. Choose **File, Export**. The Export dialog box appears. (Its exact name varies; for a table, it's Export Table '*Table Name*' To.)

3. Enter a name for the exported file. The default is the name of the object.

4. From the **Save as Type** drop-down list, choose **HTML Documents** (see Figure 27.1).

5. (Optional) If you want to use an HTML formatting template (in other words, base the export's format on that of an existing HTML file), mark the **Save Formatted** check box.

6. Click **Save**.

FIGURE 27.1   Choose HTML Documents as the type of file.

7. If you marked the **Save Formatted** check box in step 5, an HTML Output Options dialog box appears (see Figure 27.2). Enter or browse for the name of an existing HTML file on which to base the new one's formatting (if desired), and click **OK**.

FIGURE 27.2   If you selected **Save Formatted**, you can specify an HTML file on which to base the formatting.

After saving as HTML, you might want to open the saved page in your Web browser to check your work.

INSERTING HYPERLINKS INTO AN ACCESS OBJECT

There are two ways to add a hyperlink to an Access database. The first is to create a field in a table and set its data type as Hyperlink. Then any valid text string that you enter into that field becomes a hyperlink that you can click to open a specified Web page. For instance, in Figure 27.3 I'm setting up a Breeders Home Page field in my Dogs table, to hold the URLs for the home pages of the breeders from which I bought my dogs. Then, as you can see in Figure 27.4, I can enter URLs into that field which immediately become underlined hyperlinks.

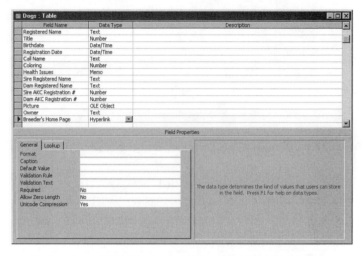

FIGURE 27.3   By setting the data type to Hyperlink, I'm telling Access that any data entered in this field is an URL.

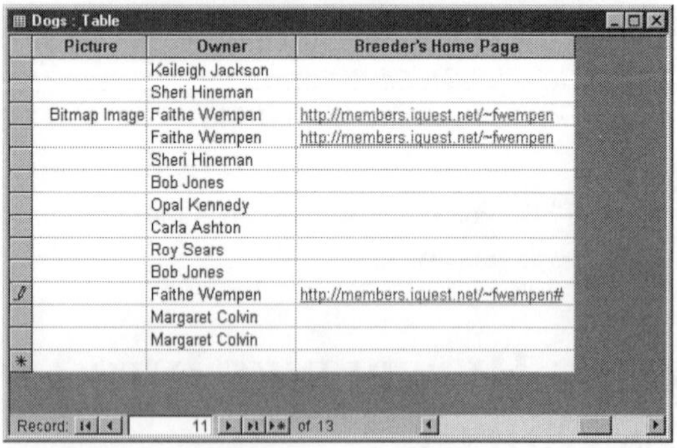

FIGURE 27.4   Any data entered into a field with a Hyperlink data type becomes a hyperlink.

Not for Web Use Only   You can hyperlink to a document on your hard disk or on your LAN instead of a Web address, if you like. For instance, if you have a supporting document for a record (such as a contract in Word for Windows), you can enter the path to the document in a hyperlink field (for instance, c:\mydocuments\contract1.doc).

The other way to set up a hyperlink is to add it to a form or report. This way, it's not associated with any particular record, but rather with the entire form or table. To do this, follow these steps:

1. Open the form or report in Design view.

2. Click the Insert Hyperlink button on the toolbar. The Insert Hyperlink dialog box appears (see Figure 27.5).

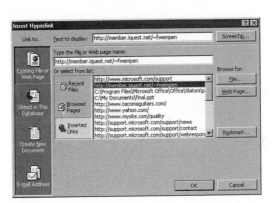

FIGURE 27.5   Specify the URL for the hyperlink in the Insert Hyperlink dialog box.

3. Enter the file or URL to hyperlink to in the **Type the File or Web Page Name** text box.

Browse for Web Pages   If you don't know the Web page address you want, click the **Web Page** button to open your Web browser, and navigate to that page. Then switch back to Access with the task bar, and the page address is entered automatically for you. To browse for non-Web files (such as a file on your hard disk), click the **File** button instead.

4. Click **OK**. Access inserts the hyperlink in the active section. You can drag to move it to any position on the form you like, just as you can move any object on a form (see Lesson 15).

The preceding method inserts a simple text hyperlink that lists the URL. If you want something fancier, you can create a picture and assign the hyperlink to it. Follow these steps to create a picture that serves as a hyperlink:

1. Insert a picture or command button in the report or form, as you learned to do in Lesson 17.

2. Right-click the picture or button and select **Properties** from the shortcut menu that appears.

3. In the properties sheet, click the **Format** tab.

4. Type the URL in the **Hyperlink Address** text box (see Figure 27.6), or click the **Build** button to open the insert Hyperlink dialog to select a URL.

5. Close the properties sheet. Now when you click the picture or button, it activates the hyperlink.

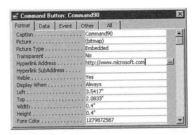

FIGURE 27.6   Specify a URL address in the **Hyperlink Address** text box and the picture becomes a hyperlinked object.

CREATING DATA ACCESS PAGES

If you've used Access in earlier versions, you may have noticed an extra "tab" or button in the database window called **Pages**. This is used to create *data access pages*.

Data access pages are specially designed Web pages that pull data from your access database and provide it on the Internet.

Data Access Pages   These are specially designed Web pages that pull data from your Access database and provide it on the Internet.

You can create a data access page in four ways:

* Create a data access page with AutoPage. Choose a record source, and AutoPage creates a page that uses all the fields from that record source.

* Create a data access page with a wizard. The wizard asks you questions about sources, fields, layout, and formatting, and creates the page based on your answers.

* Make an existing Web page into a data access page.

* Create a data access page on your own (not recommended for beginners).

The best method for beginners is AutoPage, just to see what the feature is all about. Follow these steps to use AutoPage.

1. In the database window, click **Pages**.

2. Click the **New** button. The New dialog box opens.

3. Click **AutoPage: Columnar**.

4. From the drop-down list, choose a table or query to use.

5. Click **OK**. The page appears, as shown in Figure 27.7.

6. Close the page's window. A box appears asking whether you want to save your changes.

7. Choose **Yes**. The Save As Data Access Page dialog box appears. (This way you can save it as a separate file from your database, for publishing on the Internet.)

8. Type a name in the File name box, and then choose **Save**.

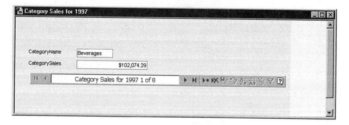

Figure 27.7   A simple data access form created in Access.

When Access saves a data access page, it also saves a folder containing the data. When you transfer the HTML file to a Web server, make sure you transfer the accompanying folder too. Then your Internet audience will be able to browse the data using their Web browsers, as shown in Figure 27.8.

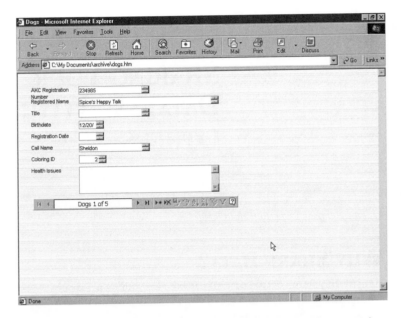

FIGURE 27.8   Your Access data, being browsed in an ordinary Web browser.

In this lesson, you learned how to connect your Access data with the World Wide Web. In the next lesson, you will learn how to share your data safely with others.

LESSON 28

SHARING YOUR DATABASE WITH OTHERS

In this lesson, you will learn how to share your data with other people without compromising your data's safety.

WHY SHARE DATA?

You probably have not created your database for your own use only. Instead, you probably created it as a tool for an entire team or even an entire company. Many people benefit from access to your data.

But you don't want to just put your database out there completely unprotected. Otherwise, an inexperienced or malicious user could make changes to it or even ruin it completely. The following sections explain how to share your data safely.

SETTING UP EXCLUSIVE USE

You can't set a password for a database (see the following section) if the database is open in Shared mode. Shared mode lets more than one person work on a database at once on a network.

By default, databases are opened in Shared mode. You can override this, and open a database in Exclusive mode, by selecting the **Exclusive** check box in the Open dialog box when you open the file.

If you want to set the default to Exclusive mode for all databases you open, follow these steps:

1. Select **Tools, Options**. The Options dialog box appears.

2. Click the **Advanced** tab.

3. In the Default Open Mode area, click **Exclusive**.

4. Click **OK**.

Why Isn't It Exclusive?   If you are reopening your database after you set the default for **Exclusive**, use the **File, Open** command. Don't pick the database from the bottom of the File menu. Why? When you open it from its name on the File menu, it opens with the same options it opened with before. If it wasn't in Exclusive mode before, it won't be now.

ASSIGNING PASSWORDS TO DATABASE FILES

The easiest way to prevent other people from making changes to your database is to assign a password to it. Anyone who doesn't know the password will be prevented from opening the file. You must have the database open in Exclusive mode (see the preceding section) to set a password for it. After you set the password for a database, users don't need to open it in Exclusive mode.

SETTING A PASSWORD

Follow these steps to set a database password:

1. Open the database that you want to protect.

2. Choose **Tools, Security, Set Database Password**. The Set Database Password dialog box appears.

3. Enter the password you want to use in the **Password** text box, and then enter it again in the **Verify** text box (see Figure 28.1). Click **OK**.

The characters you type
appear as asterisks.

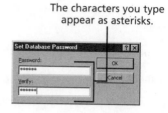

FIGURE 28.1   Passwords are case-sensitive; type it twice to make
sure you have it right.

The next time you try to open the database, a dialog box appears asking
for the password. Type it and click **OK**.

REMOVING OR CHANGING A PASSWORD

Changing the password is a two-phase process: first remove the old password, and then set a new one. Follow these steps to remove the old one,
and then follow the preceding steps to set a new one.

1. Open the database in Exclusive mode.

2. Choose **Tools, Security, Unset Database Password**. A dialog
   box appears, asking for the current password.

3. Type the current password, and then click **OK**. The password is
   now gone from the database.

USER-LEVEL SECURITY (NETWORK ONLY)

Access is designed for group use, so it has some powerful features that let
you control the access to the database by users or groups. These features
aren't useful for standalone computers; you have to be on a network.

You can use **Tools, Security, User and Group Accounts** to create pro-
files for users and groups, and then **Tools, Security, User and Group
Permissions** to give permissions for each object in the open database. See
your network administrator for help if needed.

You also can use a User-Level Security Wizard, which creates a secured database that duplicates your original and helps you set up permissions for it for your workgroup. To use it, just select **Tools, Security, User-Level Security Wizard** and follow the prompts. Figure 28.2 shows a dialog box from this wizard.

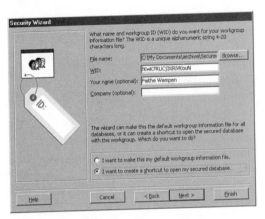

FIGURE **28.2**   The User-Level Security Wizard provides an easy way to set up user-access controls.

TEAM COLLABORATION

You can collaborate on a database project with a team in several ways:

- You can share the database file on a network by storing it in a centrally available drive and folder. Each person can access it individually and make their changes.

- You can mail a database object, such as a table, to someone via an email attachment. To do so, select the table or other object and then choose **File, Send To, Mail Recipient (as Attachment)**.

- You can use NetMeeting to hold an online or network conference.

File Format Conversion   When you mail a database object, it is converted to another file format (such as TXT or RTF), so the user might not receive what you thought you were sending. Try opening the exported file first, to see if it is close enough to the original to be worth sending.

Access 2000 enables you to use Microsoft NetMeeting, a network/online tool, to conduct meetings. In a NetMeeting meeting, you can show other meeting participants your Access file, and you can carry on a chat discussion about it in a separate window.

To start a NetMeeting conference, first make sure that NetMeeting is installed on your PC and that of everyone else who will be participating. Also make sure that all the participants have NetMeeting running. Then choose **Tools, Online Collaboration, Meet Now**. Then use the Call dialog box to invite someone to the meeting.

CREATING AN .MDE FILE

An .mde file is a database with its code stripped out, and no access to Design view. Users can enter, modify, or delete data, but they can't change the design of the database or its objects.

When your intended end users enter data into your database file, view information with a query you created, or print a report you designed, they don't need design access to the controls you used to create those objects. All they need is access to the data displayed in the controls. In fact, it's probably better that your end users don't have access to the Design views for your objects because the integrity of your database will be undermined.

.mde File   A database with its code stripped out and no access to Design view. Users can enter, modify, or delete data, but they can't change the design of the database or its objects.

When you create an .mde file from your database file, you're creating a streamlined version of the database. It has the same interface as the original, but there's no access to the design controls. Users of an .mde file can use all your forms, tables, and so on, but they can't view and modify them in Design view. Neither you nor the users can create new forms or reports. This is not only handy from a security standpoint, but it also makes the database more efficient, so it works more smoothly and quickly.

You Can't Go Back! Be very sure that the database objects' structures are exactly the way you want them before you create an .mde file. If you need to modify the design of forms, reports, or tables in a database saved as an .mde file, you must open the original database, make the changes, and then save it as an .mde file again. Any data entry done in the original .mde file must be duplicated in the new .mde file, which can be a significant amount of work.

To save a database file as an .mde file, follow these steps:

1. Open the database you want to save as an .mde file.

2. Choose **Tools, Database Utilities, Make MDE File.** The Save MDE As dialog box appears. (It's similar to a regular Save As dialog box.)

3. Enter the name you want to use for the .mde file in the **File Name** text box, and then click **Make MDE File.**

To open and use an .mde file, use the same procedure you learned for opening database files in Lesson 6 (**File, Open**), except change the **Files of Type** drop-down list to **MDE Files (*.mde).**

ENCRYPTING A DATABASE

Encryption "scrambles" the contents of a database so that it's indecipherable, even by a utility program that an expert user might employ to see your database from outside Access. If you're worried that password protection isn't enough security, you might encrypt the database as well as password protect it. You must decrypt it before you can use it again.

 Caution   Encryption only prevents people from looking at a database by using another type of program. Access users can still open and modify database objects (unless the database is secured).

 Only the Owner   If you're working in a shared file environment, such as a network, you might have access to files that you do not own. Only the owner can encrypt a database file.

To encrypt a database, follow these steps:

1. Close all databases (but leave Access open). This is important; you can't encrypt an open database.

2. Choose **Tools**, **Security**, **Encrypt/Database**.

3. In the Encrypt/Decrypt Database dialog box, choose the database file you want to encrypt. (This looks and works just like the Open dialog box.) Click **OK**.

4. In the Encrypt As dialog box, type a new name for the encrypted file. The original copy is untouched. (This looks and works just like the Save As dialog box.) Click **Save**.

Encrypting creates a new copy of the database, but the old, unencrypted version still remains. After encrypting, you will want to use Windows Explorer to find and delete the original database file on which the encrypted copy was based.

To decrypt the database, repeat the process, except choose **Tools,**
Security, Decrypt in step 2. In step 4, the dialog box will be called
Decrypt As, but the procedure is identical.

DATA PROTECTION ON FORMS

You can protect a form's individual controls from changes if you like. For
instance, I might protect the AKC Registration # field in my kennel database from changes, so that I don't accidentally overwrite these important
numbers.

To protect a field displayed in a control on a form, follow these steps:

1. Open the form in Form Design view.

2. Right-click the control and select **Properties.**

3. Click the **Data** tab.

4. Change the **Locked** property to **Yes** (see Figure 28.3).

5. Close the properties sheet.

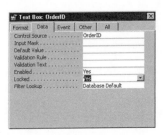

FIGURE 28.3 Protect an individual control on a form by locking it.

You can protect an entire form from changes, making it "read-only." For
instance, if you kept your company's work schedule on a form that
employees could access, you would want to keep unhappy employees
from changing their work hours. Follow these steps:

1. Open the form in Form Design view.

2. Click in the square at the intersection of the two rulers (in the
   top-left corner) to select the entire form.

3. Choose **View**, **Properties**.

4. Select the **Data** tab. To prevent changes to existing records, set **Allow Edits** to **No** (see Figure 28.4).

5. To prevent deletions of existing records, set **Allow Deletions** to **No**.

6. To prevent records from being added, set **Allow Additions** to **No**.

7. Close the properties sheet.

Click here to select the entire form.   Set **Allow Edits** to **No**.

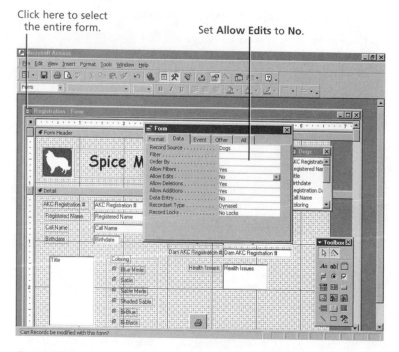

FIGURE 28.4   Control editing for the entire form from here.

In this lesson, you learned many ways to share your database. In the next lesson, you will learn how to import and export data.

LESSON 29

IMPORTING AND EXPORTING DATA

In this lesson, you will learn several ways to share Access data with other programs.

WHY IMPORT AND EXPORT DATA?

Access is great as a standalone program, but sometimes you might need to use data stored in an Access table in another program. For instance, maybe your boss wants a copy of a mailing list so he can make some cuts in it, but he's a die-hard Excel user with no interest in learning Access. You can give him the table in Excel format, and then when he's finished with it, you can import it back into an Access table.

Or perhaps you have used a different database program, such as dBASE or FoxPro, and now you want to convert your databases over to Access. You can import the data and save it in Access format.

IMPORTING DATA FROM OTHER PROGRAMS

Access accepts data from a wide variety of database programs, making it very easy to switch to Access without much loss of productivity. To import data from another program, follow these steps:

1. Open the Access database into which you want to import the data. You might want to create a new, empty database especially for this purpose (see Lesson 5).

2. Choose **File**, **Get External Data**, **Import**. The Import dialog box opens (see Figure 29.1).

FIGURE 29.1   You can import data from a variety of sources.

3. Open the **Files of Type** drop-down list and select the type of file the data is coming from. If the type you want isn't listed, rerun the Microsoft Office setup program and install the import/export filter you need.

4. Change the drive or folder to the one where the file is stored. The file's name appears in the list box in the middle of the dialog box.

 It's Not There!   If the file name doesn't appear in the list box, either you are in the wrong folder or drive, or you have selected the wrong file type.

5. Double-click the filename, or click it and then click **Import**.

Various things might happen next, depending on what type of file you're importing from. See the following sections.

IMPORTING FROM A DATABASE PROGRAM

All the database programs that Access supports imports from (Paradox and dBASE) have file formats similar enough to Access so that there's no fuss.

After you click **Import** (step 5 in the preceding steps), Access takes a moment, and then displays a message such as Successfully imported file name. That's all there is to it; the imported table appears on the Tables tab of your database.

IMPORTING FROM A SPREADSHEET

If you followed the preceding steps for a spreadsheet file, the Import Spreadsheet Wizard opens next (see Figure 29.2). Follow these steps to finish the import:

1. At the first Import Spreadsheet Wizard dialog box, click the worksheet you want to import, if there's more than one. (There are three in Figure 29.2.) A sample of it appears in the dialog box. Then click **Next.**

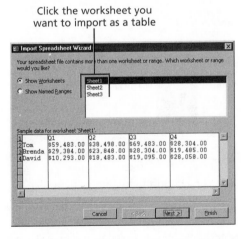

Click the worksheet you
want to import as a table

FIGURE 29.2 The Import Spreadsheet Wizard guides you through the steps of importing data from a worksheet.

Complex Worksheets If your worksheet contains anything other than columns of data (such as elaborate titles or graphics), it may not import well.

2. If the first row contains your field names, click the **First Row Contains Column Headings** check box. Click **Next** to continue.

3. Choose where you want to store your data: **In a New Table** or **In an Existing Table**. If you select **In an Existing Table**, select the table from the drop-down list. Then click **Next**.

4. Choose the names for the fields you're importing (see Figure 29.3). For the first field name, type a different title in the **Field Name** text box, if you like, and select **Yes** or **No** from the **Indexed** drop-down list. If you don't want that field at all in the imported table, select the **Do Not Import Field (Skip)** check box.

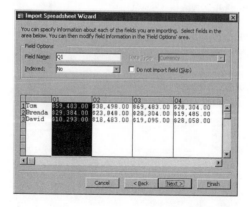

FIGURE **29.3** You can change field names if you like.

5. Use the horizontal scroll bar at the bottom of the dialog box to move the next field into view, and then click it. Then repeat step 4. Go through all the fields this way, and then click **Next** to continue.

6. You're asked to make a primary key field. If your spreadsheet has a unique column that you want to use as a primary key, click

Choose my own Primary Key and select it from the drop-down list. Otherwise, click **Let Access Add Primary Key**, or **No Primary Key**. Click **Next** to continue.

7. You're asked for a name for the table. Enter one, and then click **Finish**. Access imports the spreadsheet into your current database as a table.

8. Click **OK** at the confirmation message box to clear it. You can now see your imported table on the Tables tab of the Database window.

IMPORTING FROM A TEXT FILE

You can import data from a text file whose fields and records are delimited in some way. In other words, there is some commonly used separator character to show where one field ends and the next one begins, and where one record ends and the next record begins. You can also import from fixed-width files, if the text file contains columnar data.

In most database text files, a hard return (made by pressing **Enter**) marks the end of a record. Each record is on its own line, then. The fields of individual records are usually marked with either tabs or commas.

 Delimited   This means separated, basically. A tab-delimited database's fields are separated by tab stops; a comma-delimited database's fields are separated by commas.

If you're importing data from a text file, follow the steps at the beginning of this lesson under the heading "Importing Data from Other Programs." The Import Text Wizard opens and you can follow these steps:

1. On the first screen of the Import Text Wizard, choose **Delimited** if your text file has delimiters such as commas or tabs that separate each field. If not, you'll have to rely on spacing; choose **Fixed Width**. Click **Next** to continue.

Fixed Width   This option is for text files where the fields were set into columns by pressing the space bar. For instance, if each field were 20 spaces wide and a particular record's entry in that field took 10 characters, there would be 10 spaces before the next field's entry.

2. If you chose **Delimited**, you're asked to choose the delimiter character. Your choices are **Tab, Semicolon, Comma, Space,** or **Other** (see Figure 29.4). In the **Other** text box, you can type in any character.

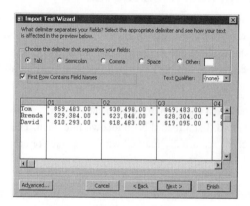

FIGURE 29.4   Choose the delimiter character, and see that Access correctly lines up the text in the right columns.

3. If the first row contains your field names, select the **First Row Contains Field Names** check box.

4. Click **Next** to continue.

5. You're asked where you want information to be stored: in a new table or an existing one. Click the **In A New Table** button, or click the **In An Existing Table** button and then select the table from the drop-down list. Click **Next** to continue.

6. In the **Field Options** box, you can change the field names for each field if you like. Enter your preferences, and then click **Next.**

7. To allow Access to create a new primary key field, click **Let Access add Primary Key**. Or specify one of the existing fields as the primary key if you prefer, or select **No Primary Key**. Click **Next**.

8. Enter a name to save the table under, and then click **Finish**. The table appears on your Tables tab.

EXPORTING DATA TO OTHER PROGRAMS

You can't export an entire Access database to another program. That's because an Access database isn't a single file; an .mdb file includes various database objects (such as Tables, Forms, Queries, Reports, and Macros) that don't translate easily into another program. Besides, if you want to export data, what you really want to export is a table. Tables in Access contain all your data. Follow these steps to export a table:

1. Open the database that contains the table.

2. Click the **Tables** tab and highlight the database you want to export.

3. Choose **File, Export**. The Export Table dialog box appears.

4. If desired, choose a different drive or folder.

5. Open the **Save As Type** drop-down list and select the file type you want (see Figure 29.5).

6. Type a name in the File Name text box to create a new file to save it in.

7. Click the **Save** button. Access saves the table in the specified format.

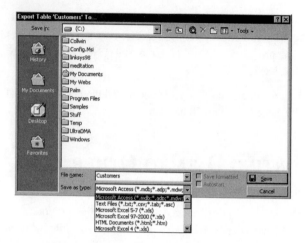

FIGURE 29.5   Export your table by saving it in a different format.

In this lesson, you learned to import and export data. In the next and final lesson, you will learn how to back up your data files so that you aren't stranded when a computer problem occurs.

LESSON 30
BACKING UP
YOUR DATA

In this lesson, you will learn how to back up your Access data for safe-keeping and how to repair damaged files.

BACKING UP YOUR DATABASE FILE

You should periodically back up your database file (that is, make a copy of it and store the copy somewhere safe), so that if anything happens to your original—such as a computer virus wiping out your hard disk contents or a fire destroying your office—your data will be retrievable.

You can back up your data to another disk in several ways:

- By using Windows Explorer, copy the database file (ends in .mdb) to a floppy disk. You should also back up System.mdw, the workgroup information file.

- Make a duplicate of the database by saving it under a different file name. Use the **File, Save As** command.

- Back up your database file by using the Backup program that comes with Windows 98. It's located in the Programs/Accessories/System Tools folder on the Start menu. If it's not there, use the Control Panel's Add/Remove Programs utility to add it. (You will need your original Windows 98 disks or CD handy.) This method should actually be your primary means of defense against disaster; you should do this for all your data files at least once a week.

LDB Files The .ldb file isn't needed. It is recreated everytime you open a database.

 Just One Table If you just want to back up a single table (or other object), import it to a new, empty database, and then back up only the new database.

REPAIRING DAMAGED DATABASE FILES

Databases can become damaged in various ways, but the most common way is through a disk error on your system. Windows 98's ScanDisk program searches for and corrects such errors; you should run this program regularly to keep your computer's file system in good repair.

You can compact and repair your current database by selecting Tools, Database Utilites, Compact and Repair Databases. If your database is seriously damaged, you may not be able to open it. In most cases, when you try to work with a damaged database, Access detects it and offers to repair the database. But if your database is damaged and Access doesn't detect it, follow these steps to repair it:

1. Close all databases.

2. Choose **Tools**, **Database Utilities**, **Compact and Repair Database**.

 Compact When a database is compacted, it's optimized to take up less storage space on your hard disk. Access does this by removing the empty spaces that deleted records, tables, or other objects once occupied, and by reorganizing the remaining database objects efficiently. In Access 2000, compacting and repairing are done at the same time; in earlier versions of the program, they were separate operations.

3. In the Database to Compact From dialog box, select the database you want to repair, and then click **Compact** (see Figure 30.1).

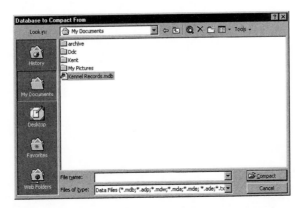

FIGURE 30.1   Select the database to compact and repair.

4. When prompted for a new file name in which to store the repaired and compacted version, enter a name. Then click **Save**.

As the database is compacting and repairing itself, you see a progress bar on the status bar. When the status bar message returns to Ready, the process is complete. Then you can open the database with the **File, Open** command.

In this lesson, you learned how to back up and repair a database. Congratulations! You have completed the last lesson in this book. You should now be able to use Access 2000 confidently.

INDEX

A

Access
  exiting, 21
  Internet, 195
  starting, 18-19
Access data file, 19
ActiveX Control command
  (Insert menu), 125
ActiveX controls, 125. *See also*
  controls
Add button, 72, 156
Add to List button (Find dialog box),
  49
adding
  calculated fields, built-in
    functions, 165
  calculated text boxes, to
    reports, 179
  controls
    forms, 100-102
    to reports, 177
  fields, 67
    calculated, 164-167
    criteria, 159-160

    to queries, 157-158
    in Table Design view, 67
  labels, 109
    to reports, 179
  tables
    Relationship window, 72
    to forms, 99
    to queries, 157
Answer Wizard, 30-31
applications
  command buttons (data-entry
    controls), 123
  Windows Paint, 131-133
arranging, controls to reports,
  178-179
AutoForms, 94-95
AutoNumber field, 60
AutoPage, data access pages, 202
AutoReport
  columnar reports, 169
  reports
    creating, 168-170
    tabular, 169
Available Fields list, 96

B

backing up database files, 221
bar charts, creating, 192-193
Blank Access database, 35
Build button, 99, 165, 200
Built-in functions, calculated fields, 165
buttons
    Add, 72, 156
    Add to List (Find dialog box), 49
    Build, 99, 165, 200
    Close, 29
    Combo Box, 119
    command, special data entry controls, 117
    Command Button, 124
    Control Wizards, 118
    Copy, 87
    Cut, 87, 158
    Delete Records, 87
    Delete Rows, 68
    Design, 65, 155
    dialog boxes, Save As and Open, 46
    divided by (/), 166
    Field List, 177
    Filter, 146
    Filter by Form, 145
    Filter by Selection, 144
    Find Now (Find dialog box), 49
    Finish, 97
    grayed out, 20
    Help, 25
    Insert, 67
    Insert Hyperlink, 199
    Insert Rows, 67
    List box, 119
    Microsoft Access Help, 24
    minus sign, 166

More, 135
New, 153
Open, 102, 151
Options, 25
Paste, 88, 165
Print, 31, 81, 153, 174, 194
Replace, 138
Run, 161
Save as Query, 146
Search, 26
Show, 28
Show Table, 72
Sort, 162
Sort Ascending, 142
Sort Descending, 142
Start, 18
Toggle Filter, 145
toolbars, 21
Toolbox, 109
Tools, 47
View, 102

C

calculated fields
    adding, 164-167
    built-in functions, adding, 165
calculated text boxes, 179
Call dialog box, 208
Cascade Delete Related Fields check box, 76
Cascade Update Related Fields check box, 76
cells, 6
    content
        changing, 83
        editing, 84
        replacing, 83
    movement keys, 85
    selecting, 83

changing. *See also* editing
  column width, 90-91
  content, cells, 83
  drives, 45
  folders, 46
  fonts, 92
  passwords, 206
  row height, 91
  tab order, 113-114
Chart Wizard, 189
charts, 189
  creating, 189
    bar, 192-193
    line, 193
    pie, 190-191
  in Print Preview, 194
  saving, 194
check boxes
  Cascade Delete Related Fields,
    76
  Cascade Update Related Fields,
    76
  Match Case, 136
  Standard Width, 91
  Underline, 93
choosing, databases, 34
clip art, 127-128
Close button, 29
Close command (File menu), 42
closing
  databases, 42
  Help, 29
  Office Assistant, 27
  Table Wizard, 54
  tables, 81
collaborating on databases, 207
Color drop-down list, 92
Column Width command
  (Format menu), 91
Column Width dialog box, 90

columnar forms, 95-97
columnar reports, 169
columns, changing, 90-91
Combo Box button, 119
combo groups, data-entry controls,
  117
Command Button button, 124
Command Button Wizard, 124
command buttons
  data-entry controls
    application, 123
    creating, 123-124
    form operations, 123
    miscellaneous, 123
    record navigation, 123
    record operations, 123
    report operations, 123
commands
  Edit menu
    Copy, 87
    Cut command, 87
    Delete, 87
    Delete Record, 87
    Find, 134
    Paste, 88
    Replace, 137
  File menu
    Close, 42
    Compact and Repair
      Database, 222
    Exit, 21
    Export, 196, 219
    Import, 214
    Open, 44
    Print, 174
    Save As, 221
    Save As Query, 146
    Save As/Export, 42
    Send To Mail Recipient,
      207

Format menu
  Column Width, 91
  Font, 92
  Hide Columns, 69
  Rename Column, 64
  Row Height, 92
Help menu
  Detect and Repair, 32
  Microsoft Access Help, 28
  Show the Office Assistant, 24
Insert menu, ActiveX control, 125
Query menu, Run, 161
Records menu
  Filter by Form, 145
  Filter Sort, 145
  Remove Filter/Sort, 142
  Sort, 142
shortcuts, toolbars, 21
Table menu, Sort, 141
Tools menu
  Online Collaboration, 208
  Relationships, 182
View menu
  Design View, 65
  Field List, 100
  Tab Order, 114
  Toolbox, 109
Compact and Repair Database command (File menu), 222
Condition drop-down list (Find dialog box), 48
Contact Management database wizard, 37
Contents (help), 28
Contents tab, 28

Control Wizards button, 118
Control-menu icon, 42
controls
  ActiveX, inserting, 125
  adding to forms, 100-102
  data-entry, 116
    combo group, 117
    command buttons, 117
    list box, 117
    option box, 117
  forms, formatting, 111
  moving, 105-106
    in groups, 106
    independent of field labels, 106
  reports, 176
    adding, 177
    arranging, 178-179
    formatting, 177
    moving, 177
    removing, 177
    resizing, 177
    selecting, 176
  resizing, 107
  selecting, 105
Copy button, 87
Copy command (Edit menu), 87
copying data, 87
creating
  calculated text boxes, 179
  charts, 189
    bar, 192-193
    line, 192-193
    pie, 190-191
  data access pages, 201
    with AutoPage, 202

data-entry controls
  command buttons, 123-124
  list boxes, 118
  option groups, 120-121
databases
  blank, 35
  with wizards, 37-40
forms, 94
  AutoForm, 95
  Form Wizard, 96-98
  from scratch, 98
  multitable, 185-186
  read-only, 211-212
graphics, 131-133
indexes, 146-147
mde files, 209
queries, 148
  multitable, 184
  Simple Query Wizard,
    149-150
relationships between tables,
  71-74
reports, 168
  AutoReport, 168, 170
  multitable, 187-188
  Report Wizard, 170-171
special data entry controls,
  combo boxes, 118
tables, 50-56
  by entering data, 63
  in Datasheet view, 63
  in Design view, 56-58
  with Table Wizard, 51-54
criteria
  fields, adding, 159-160
  queries, 159-160
Crosstab Query Wizard, 154
Currency field, 60
Cut button, 87, 158
Cut command (Edit menu), 87

D

data
  copying, 87
  entering, forms, 102-103
  exporting to other programs,
    219-220
  filtered, 143
    saving as queries, 146
  finding, 141
  importing, 213-219
    from a database program,
      215
    from spreadsheets,
      215-217
    from text files, 217-219
  moving, 87
  organizing, 141
  sorting, 141
data access pages
  creating, 201
    with AutoPage, 202
  saving, 202
Data Type column, 57
Data Type drop-down list, 57
data-entry controls, 116
  combo boxes, creating, 118
  combo group, 117
  command buttons, 117
    application, 123
    creating, 123-124
    form operations, 123
    miscellaneous, 123
    record navigation, 123
    record operations, 123
    report operations, 123
  list boxes, 117-118
  option box, 117
  option groups, 120-121

database files, 5
Database to Compact From dialog
    box, 223
database windows, 36-40
database wizards, 37-40
    Contact Management, 37
    including pictures, 39
    optional fields, including, 38
    report styles, 38
    screen display style, 38
    Switchboard window, 40
databases, 4
    backing up, 221
        with floppy disk, 221
    choosing, 34
    closing, 42
    collaborating, 207
    creating with wizards, 37-40
    damaged, repairing, 222-223
    decrypting, 211
    determining tables, 11
    encrypting, 210
    entries, 5
    Exclusive mode, 204
        setting, 205
    finding, 47-49
    hyperlinks, inserting, 198-200
    normalizing, 11-13
    objects, mailing, 207
    opening, 43
    passwords
        changing, 206
        removing, 206
        setting, 205-206
    planning design, 10
    saving, 41
        as HTML files, 196
    Shared mode, 204
    sharing, 204, 207
Databases tab, 37

datasheet forms, 95, 97
Datasheet view
    creating tables in, 63
    related tables, viewing, 183
    removing fields, 68
    switching from Design view, 62
Date/Time field, 59
Decimal Place formatting option, 60
decrypting databases, 211
Default Value formatting option, 61
Delete command (Edit menu), 87
Delete Record command (Edit
    menu), 87
Delete Records button, 87
Delete Rows button, 68
deleting. *See also* removing
    fields, 67-68
        from queries, 158
    forms, 95
    records, 87
    tables, 70
Design button, 65, 155
Design View, 98
    reports, entering, 175
    switching from Datasheet view,
        62
Design View command
    (View menu), 65
designing tables, 14-15
Desktop folder icon, 47
Detect and Repair command
    (Help menu), 32
determining
    forms, 15
    reports, 16-17
    tables, 11
dialog boxes
    Call, 208
    Column Width, 90
    Database to Compact From, 223

Edit Relationships, 74
Encrypt As, 210
Encrypt/Decrypt Database, 210
Export, 196
Export Table, 219
File New Database, 35-37
Find, 47
Find and Replace, 134-136
Font, 92
HTML Output Options, 197
Import, 214
Insert Hyperlink, 199
Insert Objects, 128
Insert Picture, 129
Microsoft Access, 19, 35
New, 36, 202
New Form, 95-98
New Query, 153
New Report, 169, 190
Office Assistant, 27
Open, 44
    buttons, 46
Options, 205
Print, 153
Replace, 138
Report Wizard, 170
Row Height, 92
Save, 41
Save As, 46
Save As Data Access Page, 202
Save MDE As, 209
Set Database Password, 205
Show Table, 72, 156, 184
Simple Query Wizard, 149
Tab Order, 114
Table Wizard, 51
Unhide Columns, 69
displaying Office Assistant, 24
divided by (/) button, 166
drawing graphics, 131-133

drives, changing, 45
drop down lists
    Color, 92
    Files of type, 129
    Match, 135
    Search, 135
    Size Mode, 131
    Tables/Queries, 149, 170

E

Edit menu
    Copy command, 87
    Cut command, 87
    Delete command, 87
    Delete Record command, 87
    Find command, 134
    Paste command, 88
    Replace command, 137
Edit Relationships dialog box, 74
editing. *See also* changing
    cells content, 84
    fields, 65-66
    relationships, 76
embedding subforms in forms,
    185-186
Encrypt As dialog box, 210
Encrypt/Decrypt Database dialog
    box, 210
encrypting databases, 210
entering
    data
        forms, 102-103
        shortcuts, 80
        tables, 63
    records in tables, 78-79
    reports in Design View, 175
    Table Design view, 65
Exclusive mode (databases),
    204-205

Exit command (File menu), 21
exiting, Access, 21
Export command (File menu), 196, 219
Export dialog box, 196
Export Table dialog box, 219
exporting data, 219-220
Expression builder, built-in functions, 165

F

Favorites folder, 47
field labels, moving, 106
Field List button, 177
Field List command (View menu), 100
Field List title bar, 101
Field Options box, 218
Field Properties pane, 66
Field Size formatting option, 60
fields, 5
    adding, 67
        calculated, 164-167
        criteria, 159-160
        queries, 157-158
    choosing, 52
    deleting, 67-68
    editing, 65-66
    formatting options, 60
        Decimal Places, 60
        Default Value, 61
        Field Size, 60
        Format, 60
        Required, 61
    hiding, 69
    including in forms, 96
    indexing, 146-147
    linking, 73
    optional, including, 38

primary keys, setting, 53-61
properties, 58-66
protecting, 211
queries
    deleting, 158
    hiding, 164
    showing, 164
    sorting, 162-163
removing, 67-68
    in Datasheet view, 68
    in Table Design view, 68
selecting
    blocks, 101
    non-adjacent fields, 101
types, 59-60
    AutoNumber, 60
    currency, 60
    date/time, 59
    Hyperlinks, 60
    Lookup Wizard, 60
    memos, 59
    numbers, 59
    OLE objects, 60
    text, 59
    Yes/No, 60
unhiding, 69
File menu
    Close command, 42
    Compact and Repair Database command, 222
    Exit command, 21
    Export command, 196, 219
    Import command, 214
    Open command, 44
    Print command, 174
    Save As command, 221
    Save As/Export, 42
    Save As Query command, 146
    Send To Mail Recipient command, 207

File New Database dialog box,
  35-37
files
    Access data, 19
    databases, 5
      reapairing damaged,
       222-223
      backing up, 221
    finding, 47
    mdb, 19
    mde, 209
    msaccess.exe, 19
    text, importing data from,
      217-219
Files of type drop-down list, 129
Filter button, 146
Filter by Form button, 145
Filter by Form command (Records
  menu), 145
Filter by Selection button, 144
filtering
    Advanced Filter/Sort, 143
    by form, 145-146
    data, 143
    records, 143-145
Find and Replace dialog box,
  134-136
Find command (Edit menu), 134
Find dialog box, 47
Find Duplicates Query Wizard, 154
Find feature, 134-137
Find Now button (Find dialog box),
  49
Find Unmatched Query Wizard, 154
Find What text box, 135-138
finding
    data, 141
    database files, 47-49
    records, 134-137
    text, 134-137

Finish button, 97
floppy disks, backing up database
  files, 221
folders
    changing, 46
    Desktop, 47
    Favorites, 47
    Help, 28
    History, 46
    My Documents, 47
    Web Folders, 47
Font command (Format menu), 92
Font dialog box, 92
Font style list box, 92
fonts, changing, 92
footers
    form, 108
    page, 108
    viewing, 108-109
Form Design view, 98-99
Form Footer, 108
Form header, 108
form operations, command buttons
  (data-entry controls), 123
Form tab, 102
Form Wizard, 94
    creating forms, 96-98
Format formatting option, 60
Format menu
    Column Width command, 91
    Font command, 92
    Hide Columns command, 69
    Rename Comlumn, 64
    Row Height command, 92
formatting
    controls
      forms, 111
      reports, 177
    tables, 89

formatting options (fields), 60
  Decimal Places, 60
  Default Value, 61
  Field Size, 60
  Format, 60
  Required, 61
Formatting toolbar, 111-112
forms, 6
  clip art, importing, 128
  columnar, 95-97
  controls
    adding, 100-102
    formatting, 111
    moving, 105-107
    resizing, 107
    selecting, 105
  creating, 94-98
    AutoForm, 95
    Form Wizard, 96-98
    from scratch, 98
  data, entering, 102-103
  datasheet, 95-97
  deleting, 95
  determining, 15
  filtering, 145-146
  graphics, importing, 129-130
  justified, 97
  modifying, 104
  multitable, creating, 185-186
  opening Form Design view, 102
  protecting, 211
  read-only, 211-212
  subforms, embedding, 185-186
  tables, adding, 99
  tabular, 95-97
Forms object type
  (Database window), 98
functions, built-in, 165

G-H

General tab, 35
  Design view, 147
graphics, 127
  drawing, 131-133
  forms, importing to, 129-130
  resizing, 130-131
grayed out buttons, 20

headers
  form, 108
  page, 108
  viewing, 108-109
Help, 23-33
  Answer Wizard, 30
  articles, 29
  closing, 29
  Contents, 28
  Detect and Repair command, 32
  folders, 28
  Index, 29-30
  Internet, 23-33
  Microsoft Web site, 33
  Office Assistant, 23-27
    asking questions, 26-27
    light bulbs, 26
    searching Help, 25
  topics
    printing, 31
    reading, 31
    selecting, 28
  What's This? tool, 23-33
Help button, 25
Help Contents window, 29
Help menu commands
  Detect and Repair, 32
  Microsoft Access Help, 28
  Show the Office Assistant, 24

Hide Columns command (Format menu), 69
hiding
  fields, 69
    in queries, 164
  Office Assistant, 24
History folder, 46
HTML (Hypertext Markup Language), 195
  files, saving, 196
HTML Output Options dialog box, 197
Hyperlink Address text box, 201
Hyperlink field, 60
hyperlinks, inserting
  in databases, 198-200
  pictures, 200
Hypertext Markup Language. *See* HTML

I

icons
  Control-menu, 42
  shortcuts, 19
Image tool, 129
Import command (File menu), 214
Import dialog box, 214
Import Spreadsheet Wizard, 215
importing
  clip art, 128
  data, 213-214
    database program, 215
    spreadsheets, 215-217
    text file, 217-219
  graphics to forms, 129-130
Importing Text Wizard, 217
including optional fields, 38
Index tab, 29

indexes
  creating, 146-147
  help, 29-30
Insert button, 67
Insert Hyperlink button, 199
Insert Hyperlink dialog box, 199
Insert menu, ActiveX Control command, 125
Insert Object dialog box, 128-132
Insert Picture dialog box, 129
Insert Rows button, 67
inserting
  ActiveX controls, 125
  hyperlinks
    to databases, 198-200
    to picures, 200
  records, 86
Internet, 195
  Help, 23-33

J-L

justified forms, 97

labels, 109
  reports, 179
landscape orientation (reports), 173
launching. *See* starting
line charts, creating, 192-193
linking fields, 73
List box button, 119
list boxes
  data-entry controls, 117
  Font, 92
  Font style, 92
  Size, 92
lists
  Available Fields, 96
  Look In, 135
  Object Type, 132
  Selected fields, 96

Look In drop-down list, 45
Look In list, 135
Lookup wizard field, 60

M

mailing database objects, 207
Main Switchboard window, 39
Match Case check box, 136
Match drop-down list, 135
mdb files, 19
mde files
    creating, 209
    saving, 209
Memo field, 59
menu bar, 20
menus, 20
Microsoft
    Access Help button, 24
    Access Help command (Help
      menu), 28
    Access Help window, 28
    Clip Gallery, 128
    NetMeeting, 207
    Web site (Help), 33
minus sign button, 166
miscellaneous command buttons
  (data-entry controls), 123
modifying
    forms, 104
    tables, 65
More button, 135
movement keys
    cells
        Control/End, 85
        Control/Home, 85
        Control/left arrow, 85
        Control/right arrow, 85
        End, 85

        Home, 85
        left arrow, 85
        right arrow, 85
    tables
        Control/down arrow, 80
        Control/End, 80
        Control/Home, 80
        Control/up arrow, 80
        down arrow, 80
        End, 80
        Home, 80
        Shift/Tab, 80
        Tab, 80
        up arrow, 80
moving
    controls, 105-106
        groups, 106
        independent of fields, 106
        reports, 177
    data, 87
    fields labels, 106
    Office Assistant, 24
    tables, 80
msaccess.exe file, 19
multitable
    forms, 185-186
    queries, 184
    reports, 187-188
My Documents icon, 47

N

NetMeeting, 207-208
New button, 153
New dialog box, 36, 202
    General tab, 35
New Form dialog box, 95, 98
New Query dialog box, 153
New Report dialog box, 169, 190

normalizing
    databases, 11-13
    rules
        *avoiding redundant data,
        13*
        *avoiding repeated
        information, 12*
Number field, 59

O

Object Type list, 132
objects, shortcuts, 37
Office Assistant, 23-27
    asking questions, 26-27
    closing, 27
    displaying, 24
    help bubble, 25
    hiding, 24
    light bulbs, 26
    moving, 24
    searching Help, 25
Office Assistant dialog box, 27
OLE (object linking elements)
    controls, inserting, 125
    Object field, 60
Online Collaboration command
    (Tools menu), 208
Open button, 102, 151
Open command (File menu), 44
Open dialog box, 44
    buttons, 46
    shortcuts
        Desktop icon, 47
        Favorites icon, 47
        History icon, 46
        My Documents icon, 47
        Web Folders icon, 47

opening
    databases, 43
    forms, Form Design view, 102
    queries, in Query Design view,
        155
    Relationships window, 182
option box, data-entry controls, 117
option groups, data-entry controls,
    creating, 120-121
options, referential integrity, 74
Options button, 25
Options dialog box, 205
Or tab, 146
organizing data, 141

P

Page Footer, 108
Page Header, 108
passwords, databases
    changing, 206
    removing, 206
    setting, 205-206
Paste button, 88, 165
Paste command (Edit menu), 88
pictures. *See also* clip art
    database wizards, 39
    graphics, 127
    hyperlinks, inserting in, 200
pie charts, creating, 190-191
planning database designing, 10
portrait orientation (reports), 173
primary keys, setting, 53-54, 61
Print button, 31, 81, 153, 174, 194
Print command (File menu), 174
Print dialog box, 153
Print Preview
    charts, 194
    reports, viewing in, 174

printing
    Help topics, 31
    query results, 152
    reports, 174
    tables, 81
programs. *See* applications
properties, fields, 58-66
Property drop-down list (Find dialog
    box), 48
protecting forms, 211

Q

queries, 8
    creating, 148
        Simple Query Wizard,
        149-150
    criteria, 159-160
    fields
        adding, 157-158, 184-187
        deleting, 158
        hiding, 164
        showing, 164
        sorting, 162-163
    filtered data, saving as, 146
    multitable, creating, 184
    Query Design view
        opening in, 155
        starting in, 156
    rerunning, 151
    results, 152
        printing, 152
        viewing, 150, 161
    saving, 151
    select, 149
    tables, adding, 157
Queries tab, 149
Query Design view, 155
Query menu, Run command, 161
query wizards, 153

R

read-only forms, creating, 211-212
reading Help topics, 31
record navigation command buttons
    (data-entry controls), 123
record operations command buttons
    (data-entry controls), 123
records, 5
    deleting, 87
    entering, 78-79
    filtering, 143-145
    finding, 134-137
    inserting, 86
    replacing, 137-138
    selecting, 85
    selection symbols, 86
    sorting, 141-142
Records menu
    Filter by Form command, 145
    Remove Filter/Sort command,
        142-145
    Sort command, 142, 162
referential integrity, 75
    options, 74
    setting, 76
related tables, 181
    viewing in Datasheet view, 183
relationships
    creating, 71-74
    editing, 76
    removing, 77
    tables, 181
Relationships command (Tools
    menu), 182
Relationships window, 72, 182
Remove Filter/Sort command
    (Records menu), 145

removing
    controls, 177
    fields, 67-68
        in Datasheet view, 68
        in Table Design view, 68
    passwords, 206
    relationships, 77
Rename Column command
  (Format menu), 64
repairing damaged database files,
  222-223
Replace button, 138
Replace command (Edit menu), 137
Replace dialog box, 138
Replace With text box, 138
replacing
    content, cells, 83
    records, 137-138
    text, 137-138
report operations command buttons
  (data-entry controls), 123
Report Wizard, 170-171
reports, 6
    AutoReport, 168-170
    calculated text boxes, 179
    columnar, 169
    controls, 176
        adding, 177
        arranging, 178-179
        formatting, 177
        moving, 177
        removing, 177
        resizing, 177
        selecting, 176
    creating, 168-170, 187-188
    Design View, 175
    determining, 16-17
    labels, 179
    printing, 174
    Report Wizard, 170-171

    styles, 38
    tabular, 169
    viewing Print Preview, 174
Required formatting option, 61
rerunning queries, 151
resizing
    controls, 107
        in reports, 177
    graphics, 130-131
results queries, 152
    printing, 152
    viewing, 150, 161
Row Height command (Format
  menu), 92
Row Height dialog box, 92
rules, normalization, 12
    avoiding redundant data, 13
    avoiding repeated information,
      12
Run button, 161
Run command (Query menu), 161

S

Sample Fields list (Table Wizard), 52
Sample Tables list (Table Wizard),
  51
Save As command (File menu), 221
Save As Data Access Page dialog
  box, 202
Save As dialog box
    buttons, 46
    shortcuts, 46
        Desktop icon, 47
        Favorites icon, 47
        History icon, 46
        My Documents icon, 47
        Web Folders icon, 47
Save As Query button, 146

Save As Query command (File
  menu), 146
Save As/Export command (File
  menu), 42
Save dialog box, 41
Save In drop down list, 45
Save MDE As dialog box, 209
saving
  charts, 194
  data, filtered, 146
  data access pages, 202
  databases, 41
    as HTML files, 196
  files, mde, 209
  queries, 151
ScreenTips, 21
Search button, 26
Search drop-down list, 135
searching Help
  Index, 30
  Office Assistant, 25
security, user and group permissions,
  206
Selected Fields list, 96
selecting
  cells, 83
  controls, 105
    on reports, 176
  fields
    blocks, 101
    non-adjacent, 101
  Help topics, 28
  records, 85
selection symbols, records, 86
Send To Mail Recipient command
  (File menu), 207
Set Database Password dialog box,
  205

setting
  databases
    Exclusive mode, 205
    passwords, 205-206
  primary keys, 53-54, 61
  referential integrity, 76
Shared mode (databases), 204
sharing databases, 204-207
shortcuts
  Design View, 65
  Desktop icon, 47
  entering data, 80
  Favorites icon, 47
  History icon, 46
  icons, 19, 46
  My Documents icon, 47
  Objects, 37
  Web Folders icon, 47
Show button, 28
Show Table button, 72
Show Table dialog box, 72, 156, 184
Show the Office Assistant command
  (Help menu), 24
showing fields in queries, 164
Simple Query Wizard, 149-150
Size list box, 92
Size Mode drop-down list, 131
sizing
  columns, 90-91
  rows, 91
Sort Ascending button, 142
Sort button, 162
Sort command
  Records menu, 162
  Table menu, 141
Sort Descending button, 142
sorting
  data, 141
  fields in queries, 162-163
  records, 141-142

spreadsheets, importing data from, 215-217
Standard Width check box, 91
Start button, 18
starting
  Access, 18-19
  NetMeeting, 208
  queries in Query Design view, 156
  Table Design view, 56
status bar, 20
subforms, embedding, 185-186
switching between Design and Datasheet view, 62

T

tab order, changing, 113-114
Tab Order command (View menu), 114
Table Datasheet view, 54
Table Design view, 54-56
  adding fields, 67
  entering, 65
  removing fields, 68
  starting, 56
Table menu, Sort command, 141
Table Wizard, 50-54
tables, 5
  adding to Relationship window, 72
  cells, 6
    changing content, 83
    replacing content, 83
  closing, 81
  creating, 50-63
    in Datasheet view, 63
    in Design view, 56-58
    with Table Wizard, 51-54
  deleting, 70

  designing, 14-15
  determining, 11
  fields, 5
    adding, 67
    choosing, 52
    deleting, 67-68
    editing, 65-66
    formatting options, 60-61
    hiding, 69
    properties, 58-66
    types, 59-60
    unhiding, 69
  formatting, 89
  forms, 99
  modifying, 65
  movement keys
    Control/down arrow, 80
    Control/End, 80
    Control/Home, 80
    Control/up arrow, 80
    down arrow, 80
    End, 80
    Home, 80
    Shift/Tab, 80
    Tab, 80
    up arrow, 80
  moving in, 80
  primary keys, setting, 53-54, 61
  printing, 81
  queries, 157
  records, 5
    entering, 78-79
  related, 181-183
  relationships
    creating, 71-74
    editing, 76
    removing, 77
  shortcuts, entering data, 80
  themes, 14
Tables tab, 54

Tables/Queries drop-down list, 96,
    149, 170
tablular forms, 95
tabs
    Answer Wizard, 31
    Contents, 28
    Databases, 37
    Form, 102
    General, 35
    General (Design view), 147
    Index, 29
    Or, 146
    Queries, 149
    Tables, 54
tabular forms, 97
tabular reports, 169
    AutoReport, 169
text
    finding, 134-137
    replacing, 137-138
Text Box tool, 179
text boxes
    calculated, creating, 179
    Column Width, 91
    Find What, 135, 138
    Hyperlink Address, 201
    Replace With, 138
Text field, 59
themes, tables, 14
title bars, Field List, 101
Toggle Filter button, 145
toolbars, 20-21
    command shortcuts, 21
    Formatting, 111-112
    Microsoft Access Help button,
        24
Toolbox button, 109
Toolbox command (View menu),
    109

tools
    Formatting Toolbar, 111-112
    Image, 129
    Text Box, 179
    Unbound Object, 128
Tools button, 47
Tools menu
    Online Collaboration command,
        208
    Relationships command, 182
ToolTips, 21

U-V

Unbound Object tool, 128
Underline check box, 93
Unhide Columns dialog box, 69
unhiding fields, 69
URL (Uniform Resource Locator),
    196
    hyperlinks, inserting in
        databases, 198-200
user and group accounts security,
    206
user and group permissions, 206
user-level security, 206
User-Level Security Wizard, 207

View button, 102
View menu
    Design View command, 65
    Field List command, 100
    Tab Order command, 114
    Toolbox command, 109
viewing
    footers, 108-109
    headers, 108-109
    query results, 161
    related tables in Datasheet view,
        183
    reports, Print Preview, 174

views
   Datasheet
      creating tables in, 63
      removing fields, 68
   Design, 98-99
   Form Design, 98
   Query Design, 155
   switching between, 62
   Table Datasheet, 54
   Table Design, 54, 56
      entering, 65
      removing fields, 68

W-Z

Web Folders icon, 47
Web. *See* Internet
What's This? tool, 23-33
windows. *See also* views
   database, 36-40
   Help Contents, 29
   Main Switchboard window, 39
   Microsoft Access Help, 28
   Relationships
      adding tables, 72
      opening, 182
Windows Paint program, 131-133
wizards, 8
   Answer, 30
   Chart, 189
   Command Button, 124
   Crosstab Query, 154
   databases, 38
      creating, 37-40
      pictures, 39
      report styles, 38
      screen display style, 38
      Switchboard window, 40
   Find Duplicates Query, 154

Find Unmatched Query, 154
Import Spreadsheet, 215
Importing Text, 217
Lookup, 60
queries, 153
Report, 170-171
Simple Query, 149-150
Table, 50-54
User Level Security Wizard, 207
work area, 20
WWW (World Wide Web). *See* Internet

Yes/No field, 60

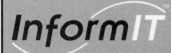